AF473400

Lyrical and *Lovely* Thoughts

POEMS

J. Kirby Smith

authorHOUSE®

AuthorHouse™
1663 Liberty Drive
Bloomington, IN 47403
www.authorhouse.com
Phone: 1 (800) 839-8640

Published by AuthorHouse 04/18/2016

ISBN: 978-1-4634-4538-6 (sc)
ISBN: 978-1-4634-4537-9 (hc)
ISBN: 978-1-4634-4536-2 (e)

Library of Congress Control Number: 2011914327

Print information available on the last page.

This book is printed on acid-free paper.

Contents

Dedication

I would love so very much to dedicate this book to quite simply the very best friend and dearest sweetheart I will ever know-the former Cheryl Renee Fox—My indispensable and wonderful wife.

The Vicissitude Of The Storm

Madness as a quality incorporates with calm
Be it not a soothing balm for the black widow
Kills without a qualm from out her indolence
Hear the stillness stalk with virulence in its rush!
The gossamer threads no longer brush
My forehead wafting by I feel the hush
Of a most voluminous silence
Turpid clouds abounding form vast quasi things
While the robin wings away
Ridden from the darkening day
I feel the storm!
Whose harbinger airs are heavy and warm
The poplar shivering blends her nuance
Of the storm's malign pursuance
Pounding down tempestuously the rains!
Plummet to the mundane plains
Thunder claps discordant!
With the violent torrent
Tremble down and pierce and mingle!
While the scathing shrill winds tingle!
Heart and spine who lie supine
Amid the storm

The zenith of the storm
The rains subside
Lilies laved now sparkle side by side in the sun
Crickets chirping Rainbows pied portend the storm is done
Halcyon skies not rampant anymore
From the tempest's downpour
Twinkle down tranquility from above
Birds and bees and nature's love
Cleansing sultry climes sedate

How the storm doth renovate!
High above amidst the lull
Wings the gull
But a minute panorama
Of the storms ensuing drama
Flown in beauty so we see ineffably
The vicissitude of the storm

Swift are the gentle rains that fall in April
On the acumen of my memory stores that stir me
In tenderest thoughts or memories that chill
My being because they inundate so hauntingly

Shrill are the winds of April blowing listlessly
Like a heart unfulfilled, as yet, and full of rue
That wanders around the world seeking endlessly
A fullness and understanding to renew

My heart remembers so many Aprils
And precise little things from the past that leave me pangs
So heavy they weigh and yet they are so subtle
They stab at my heart like fangs

Oh, I bleed this month; there is something in the air
That recalls fresher happenings and beginnings in my life
Simple times that seemed easier to bear
And a breathless holding hands with my ex-wife

One certain special day with her—many Aprils ago
When the clouds were turgid and welling
The day was windy and it was Sunday
And my heart was swelling

I see shadows on windows and walls of the past
Within rooms where the people have vanished
The rooms seem so vivid; their details last
In my mind not a corner's been banished

And some of the rooms have meant love affairs gone
The past is a terrible burden
The sum of its weight makes me tired and wan
The present is certainly sudden

Oh, but April you are so fresh; so sweet
Although too often bittersweet to me
Is it possible, yet, that I might meet
The love that will set me free

Dear April, I love you even though it hurts
And I am getting wearier with the years
And I'm trying; I'm trying; my heart still exerts
Through a cavalcade (oh, a cavalcade) of tears

There May Come A Day

When all the men and mystic maidens
Of my day begin to wizen,
This heart will be heavy-laden
To face a dark horizon.

Should I outlive my peers
The fields of clover won't be sweet again,
I'll walk through them alone in those years,
Thinking of what's been.

It saddens me to think of such a thing.
So gladly I face each new dawn,
A song in my heart to sing
Before they're gone.

I want to taste life's sweetness
And accept every man as he is,
Before death's fleetness
Let him have what's his.

Yes, let me kiss my maidens and
Others too; let us breathe the roses,
Rejoicing together till the end.
(And may there be love between us.)

Trillion Year Picnic

We have come beyond time to a new time!
Conducive to new things and hearts unlike gneiss
With celerity it has so changed that this clime
Is an attar sweet isle and spice!

For Whirlwind! He hath destroyed all that was
In acanthus like prickles of wrath
The polemics of man have been ended because!
He tired of hate and their blood baths

For Whirlwind destroyed the world, vitiating war.
He destroyed it with seething shrill winds!
Shrieking tempestuous winds to the core
Of the planet emended all sin!

And only the relics of worth have been saved
The pyramid tombs of the Pharaohs
Or such as the durable highways so paved
In the States or the wondrous Greek porticos

The acropolis, yes, and the Parthenon live
And some strong vaulted structure of Rome
Parmenidean logic, the sweet poems of Ovid
The cabin that Lincoln made home

But beyond this his wrath like a scimitar blade
Shrieked rue o'er the earth with deep terror
Whining and wailing invectives he made
From his lofty tempestuous dormer

And all men weeped their agony!
The splenetic shrieking Whirlwind
Inveighed the world in symphony
An incessant and horrible din!

The eerie wailing devastated all!
Sobbing through deserts and countries
Its sobbing made skyscrapers fall
And deteriorate in the cities

Inciting the night with prolific sensations
He scattered all evil from Earth
He leveled all sin from the nations
But then there was a new birth!

The few he Favored hovered from his sorcery
To scintillate the darkness with their spirit
Beloved kindred spirits; would they now be free
Of pain!? If only Whirlwind would grant it

And they hovered in the caves of time in darkness!
Like egrets lost and beauteous and blithe
From Whirlwind's immediate pursuance
Their number form the whole far less than tithe

And all ended in stupendous silence!
Whirlwind's wrath was propitiated!
Because their innocence had ended his suspense
And it made his momentum languid

The arias of wind became serenity
The caves of time were exited, the land
Was calm, they now with Whirlwind had repartee!
He talked with them and offered his remand

Though violent and strong he still was sapient
And offered for their innocence his mercy
If only they would stand to be compliant
And live in love and empathetic harmony

They huddled in their raggedness before him
Like palfreys who but want to please their master
But none the less they questioned him for all seemed dim
The whole of Earth was shrouded in disaster!

The cryptic land was bleak and dark and shrouded
Eternal night was here from man's attack
With debris and with soot the sun was clouded
And even in the noon the sky was black!

They questioned this, the whole of pantheism
Seemed ruined for if God were in all things
How could they have the vaguest predilection
For life if this is what the landscape brings!

Anathema was everywhere and ruin
A nightmare was the land, a smoking hell
A target ground it seemed for bolts of Odin
In unison they questioned . . . all is well?!

The time machine! A flash of light
Unveiled it before them with a sound
Of thunder which illumined all the night
And made each last survivor's heart beat pound!

The time machine in surpassing wonder!
Was lain before them, now, within their visage
And still the skies were echoing their thunder!
As Whirlwind put forth this vibrant message!

Go now into the time machine my brothers!
And languish for this place in time no more
Like ether it will help block out the others
From your mind; the grief; you'll open other doors!

And immediately when they had got inside it
It whirled and flexed and sparkled like a gem
Like an elevator ride all brightly lit
(a gnome of anaesthesia, it led them)

Chimerical and wonderful the adventurers were
Like tendrils clinging desperate to a reef
Until a violent jolt and a visual blur
Expulsed them and they stared in disbelief!

The river styx was not what brought them here!
'Twas tantamount to heaven or its wild imaginings!
The fragrances of incense, clove, and clover
Excited and prepared for incredible happenings!

But how could they, now, in all their dreams prepare?!
The sounds of tambourines were everywhere
Where grass might be were carpets of velour
This sanguine land intoxicated cares

It made them hopeful; they forgot their cares
But yet it made them purposeful with foresight
With discretion or abandon, incredible dares
Were made by them with subtlety or might!

The skies and all of nature were a sunshine
And everything was vibrant; filled with God
The waters were the colour of a wine
That mellowed them; In work they did not plod!

And everyone worked together very well
And loved with an abandon; (but Minerva's wisdom)
Made its measure ell in reason; hills and vales
Resounded with this new kinetic kingdom

Looking Out Over The City From Way Up Here

Memories can be given in a wisp of wind
On a wintry day near the park
Especially a lonely day in focus from above
The city in my apartment, here, near dark

And memories can be added
With the shadow's approbation
Which linger with the whisperings of twilight
Upon the city; an apparition

Indefinable things like scents
Upon the wind of ashes burning
Recalling other scents of roasts and youth
Lonely then; my hearts' still yearning

The tennis court, the park, in barren quiet
Litter on the ground or wafting by
The shrill train whistle distant, bleak, and lonely
All have known the feeling with a sigh

Nameless cars and people on the pavements
Passing by like rain upon the heart
Kids who'se mirth and spirit that I envy
Spinning by like gnomes they run and dart

The buildings that overshadow everything
Adamant and hard they almost seem
Grim because they focus not on people
Seemingly I see them in a dream

The city seems a dream from way up here
Impassive dark and so surrealistic
A pattern that's gestault and is unbroken
Not to be deciphered, brick by brick

The people, molecules in a mass of jelly
Screamingly apparent with the street lights
But a moment then they pass forever
Spots upon the pavements put to flight

People, cars, and buildings seem as shadows
Almost unrelatable, they seem
(I look down on fire escapes, alleys, secret nooks)
Eerie lights in pallor seem to scream

The apathy, the crime, the alienation
Can be beaten if we put aside our fear
And mold our city more with an affection
For people; this is obvious from here

The Colours Of Rodney

A man's attitude in part
Is shaped by his rambling boyhood
Much of the fabric of his heart
That is understood

And the fabric of Rodney
Was one of optimism
His colours showed to me
Like the many of a prism

Especially his summer green
Flights of fancy in our playing
His attitude was keen
When the August skies were graying

Never did he criticize
Or complain about the useless
His eyes were gleaming eyes
Always binding us

That heart, I felt, was gold
And reckless abandon
Forgetting himself he was bold
To help a companion

Red was the colour of Rodney
In torment to light up the sky
His fiery eyes could see
Easily through a lie

But always there was that white
In the innocent heart he had
Forgiving all things in his sight
(No matter how bad)

Little Memories But Big

I am a man who sometimes remembers
The little things of life that are so sweet
Of shadowy, shadowy Decembers
Lights amid the valleys, flakes, and people
So long ago . . . so fleet

And I am a man who sometimes encountered
Terrible pain and misunderstandings but yet
Though there have been moments when I've floundered
I have gotten up to see those little things
(With no regret)

My Mother's smile when I was a lad
Certain happy little moments with friends
Those special little moments of rapport; of glad
When I and at least one other person in a room shared empathy
(Our wavelengths are attuned; our hearts distend)

When the mood has been reflective and shared
Or silly and shared with a wild abandon
But the attitude was, we cared
Though unsaid and merely felt, of course
When hearts were one

Fragmented moments of a long ago picnic
When Uncle George was still here
His smile; the light from a candle wick
That has gone out and faded to the grave
Leaving but a tear

So many nuances of things when I was a kid
Interspersed moments people emotions
When my heart was volcanic amid
Those growing pains of youth
Long ago, so many Suns

Even the shadowy recesses of the rooms
That I walked in as a lad
And of other houses and long ago fields
That I roamed so careless, now gone
Yes, truly sad

A moment in the army shared on duty
Or with a friend in childhood
Nocturnal quiet shorelines . . . coming on lonely . . .
I'll never forget; I'll never forget
The bad; the good

The Cards: A Parable [Humor]

Flitted merrily in menthol air
In Roseate flair the queen
Atop the dais tabletop a sedentary scene
Athwart the cards, pernicious pawns of fate
Skips ornate while contenders lie in wait, Poignant keen
Obsequious of chance, libations offered from their wine
Which they swill and spill as servants, leonine
Contiguous to one another there
Invidious they are; Iscariot expressions that they wear

Pulling lustily the winner, there
Omnipotent share his take
An outside straight filled by an ace illuminates his face
Enamored thus prosaic be his play
Without volition so his soul be gay—to erase
Propitiate or quell—dispel the tumult of his foes
Lest their passions flow in Satan's scarlet throes
Lo spurious! His methods be not fair
Iniquitous they are; The burden of their hatred that they bear

Shuffled fervidly neath neon lights
Cadaverous cards reflect
Of somber play, the face cards they, in poses they select
Irradiate the rays received and cast
Them back in glints portray themselves aghast, ghastly white
Approbrious of vice, their use; Unravel they the deuce
To chagrin their grim tormentors with abuse
Mercurial, ah fickle as the wind
All treasures they rescind; Vindictive of their masters who have sinned

Clasping furtively his rapier, he
Defiantly it is drawn
Held high in might and majesty behind his royal crown
The king who'se grim decorum seems to show
That he who lives by sin alone shall know!—Sudden woe

A dagger drawn at once! Of him who hath lost all this nonce!
And retaliate they all, dread response
(Found, lying there upon the floor; All slayed)
Atop the deck still laid—Their grim and ghastly seer; The ace of spades

Your "One" True Love

The eternal night seems not eternal
And all the many flowers of the forests
That are piquant now all seem converged on you
While snuggled on the heaven of her breasts
(Your spirit rests)

All the struggles of your heart are lessened
Eternity is now to grasp and hold
You are not a nameless fragment with no end
Your future has a purpose to unfold
(You feel bold)

You are centered and you're organized now
All meaning has been given to your life
And the phobias that plague have run afoul
Those murky thoughts that cut you like a knife
(And worsened strife)

For her penetrating mind is grasping yours
And just to know that someone understands
It's like walking miles, peaceful, on the shore
Or one but not alone through many lands
(You're in her hands)

Even if your life should pass tomorrow
It troubles not, you know you're understood
(Yes, your mind's been known) this eases any sorrow
For her you'd block a bullet if you could
(Oh yes your would)

Yes, she understands your mind and likes it!
With understanding empathy so keen
But there's something even better (quite a bit)
It's the tenderness and love that you have seen
(So like a dream)

For the stuff within her heart is greater
Than even all her empathy you've known
It's a breathless thing inside so deep and tender
It's the little girl side of her she's shown
(You're not alone)

Deeper Is My Dream

While my tranquility here
Among the eucalyptus—and the dawn
Retracts me to a year
Of love that now is gone
Her presence seems so near

Amid the river breeze's
Reminiscent sigh
How I feel it teases
Telling me goodbye
(So like her words that freed us)

Quiet were embraces
That we used to steal
How my heart beat races
Thinking of how real
(Seemed the love upon our faces)

Onward though the current
Rushes so downstream
Finding no deterrent
'Midst the spots unclean
Never there's adjournment

Nature's not unfeeling
Ever it's a guide
To a deeper meaning
Always at our side
If were only seeing

Farther down my stream
I will seek attainment
I have merely seemed
True love I've not found yet
(Deeper is my dream)

Lingerings

A certain smile, contained by the wind
The cool dark whisperings of a lonely mood at sunset
A voice within your mind beckoning beckoning, beckoning
You home. Home where the sunset touches above the eaves, faintly
Thyme; the meadows and the fields
Fragrant, soft in summer memories
Inspirited vibrations, another hour
Lushious fresh, in recollection
Igneous thought interposed by time
Time; the meadows and the fields
Flashing on, beloved only
Lugubrious made reconciled—by time
Tremulous heart on summer night
Visavis the fears and trembling
Love a figment or a thought
Or a spectre; not a happening?
Wistful images adoring
Perfect thought of what might be
Someone sweet and filled with empathy
Myriad nuances—you see

Lola

Beauty in my mind's eye
Is long forgotten simple things
A girl sweet or shy
A memory of spring

Happiness to me
Is someone who will understand
And see when none will see
Or hold an outcast's hand

Spring had lost its fragrance
Divorce had broke our bond
Although our love had once
Seemed a magic wand

Leaving me I guess
Her cold and distant words
Chilled me like the loneliness
Of a flight of winter birds

The blame was mine, Tis clear
But when a man is broken
His words can be sincere
And also quite outspoken

It was in April
That cloudy windswept day
Lola warmed the chill
Of a heart so bleak and grey

Because her mellow
Comforting and mirth
Made believe this fellow
Hadn't lost all worth

Lola tried to stem
My anguish from the start
Refusing to condemn
And heard me with her heart

A touch again of spring
She brought for me, a while
And helped remove the sting
With her smile

Spring Rain — Lost Love — Memories

Oh the pretty girls dancing by in April
Winsome and articulate, they run
And their countenances almost dim the sun
Yes, their radiance to most would overfill
But there's dark clouds, now, appearing in the sky
And I look beyond the girls, my horizon
Is filled with things that only make me cry

Oh, the storm clouds, now, are filling up the skyline
And they are above and also everywhere
Like my thoughts, within, intolerable to bear
And the substance in my head all made of wine
And the girls though so radiant they are
Even they can't quell my memories; a nightmare
That burn my mind and stick to it like tar

For although there's many others very pretty
And they fill the streets and sometimes overflow
I am bound by recollection love and woe
For there's only one with whom I've shared my memories
And there's dark clouds, now, all over in the sky
In concordance with the rain I'm hurting so
I'm asking the horizon, tell me why?

Oh, the pretty girls dancing by in April
They can't even pacify my mind
Though a few are even tolerant and kind
And the rain's consistent with my tears which spill
Yes, there's dark clouds, now, all over in my sky
For I cannot leave the memories behind
I'm filled with things that only make me cry

That Youth Of Flaming Heart Long Ago

That youth of flaming heart, years ago
When my bosom crackled over with its vim
And energy and hope and higher hurts
That yet subsided quicker than the hurts I know
Now, because of age weary pessimism

Yes, then I could race the lake waves
Without pausing to consider the serpents
And bounce back quicker then because there seemed ideals
That my soul still craves
But is that spirit spent?

The resilience came from believing
These ideals could be achieved
And held on to in some permanent solid way
In this there was a healing
Because, then, I totally believed

But yes, there have been traumas since the yore
Terrible hurts, melancholias and depressions
That I've seen in my life and others
(The hurt is even worse to view in others)
And I have grown much wearier with the seasons

But yes, oh yes, I'd like to partly hold
That youth of flaming heart of so long ago
And the stark breathtaking beauty of even some
The tears wash at this thought for I'm more old
And often all I see is hidden woe

But lord, I'd like to save some if I can
And if not for myself give some to others
(try to infuse some warmth in other's lives)
And if it fails with me to rise up then
And hold that glow in someone who is younger

For is it never true the ideal means something
If only of itself; the effort made
In attempting to banish the melancholy
In these lonesome years to try at least to bring
The joy of life to those who are afraid?

Is it not impossible to lighten
The burdens of this life by giving hope
And laughter and a quality of spirit
And maybe to your own hurt spirit brighten
(With some burning heart of youth from long ago)

The Spider Has No Soul

The breeze in its tenacity
Fails to hurt the web
That moves but does not break
Yet, it's woven delicately
And a creature amid its pattern
Sedentary and snug
Is stationed quietly.

Softly, oh so softly
A horsefly touches the web
And sticks and is pursued
By something ghastly
A horror to that insect
A horror, too, to me
A grim monstrosity.

The spider quickly glides
Pursuing with ferocity
It pounces on its prey
Entombing it and biting till it dies
Exploding in a scene to chill the mind
And rapidly retreats to where it was
Again it hides.

Yes, faster is my heart beat
It quickens with the murmer of the wind
Is all of life as cruel?
A monster that no man can ever defeat
Is it like the spider?
Luring and inducing to destroy
And then retreat.

Thinking of this though
And knowing inhumanities persist
And should not, no, but yet
The lessons that we learn from life, I know
Prove that guile and treachery are shallow
That love must be the answer
Love has soul.

Evanescent recollections iridescent seas
Recede as do the tempest midst the cool breeze
Pour forth nought sad uncertainties; Potpourri of my mind
A new brew be her wine; taste sublime

Lymphatic ebbing tides disperse. Lucidly her charms
Dispel all but adagio waves; she holds me in her arms
Across the quiet shores of time, white cygnet, placid fawn
Accrue the pale night then are gone

Effulgence born of stars descends; her lovely face a sheen
Abeyance? Now or never? Curt image my queen?
On any silent silver shore her soul does mesmerize
A token of her eyes and her sighs

Effervescent revelations, omnipotent bliss!!
Accede as do the heavens of her tender kiss
Effuse excrescent euphony; these shores a tender shrine
Flow like the river Rhine. So divine

Quiescent amaranths ascend; truculently their colour;
Avow eternal tenderness, acquiescent flower
Imbue incense and sacred rites of hyacinth her hair!
A tonic to her hair; fragrant air

Quitesssence, rendez-vous cross time; supernally her grace
Regalia be her length of tress fell down on ivory lace
Sapphire skies. Her tender eyes rescind the hoary shore
Intrepid visage, Oh my love, to quell the ocean's roar

Ubiquitous apparitions, melancholy torn
Recess as do the ocean's tempestuous storm;
Ascend on wings of rhapsody, they serenade the night
Translucent wings of light out of sight

Lorinda

Oh how I remember her
Dear God how I recall her. Assuaging breezes wisped her near
While moonlight played upon her hair
In autumn and in winter
Lorinda's raven hair.

We waltzed; we waltzed once whimsical
Withal the woodland warblers
Which winged in repertoire afar, in resonance afar.

Amid the morning marigolds, She mildly held my hand
'Twas reticence of the woods; I deemed, made quietude the land

We were wondrous wide eyed whilst we lept the forest rills
Through somnolent summer meadows, We assailed the summer hills
Here, I picked her summer daffodils

Withering wan leaves, wet sleets in autumn washed her nearer
Whilst autumn leaves wisked yonder sear and wane
My beloved I held dearer—
For her rectitude seemed clearer; Twas her innocence a mirror in the rain
Dear Lorinda ever purer in the rain

And she whispered soft and silently
She'd seek her love eternal; One like me
And stroll with him in ecstasy amidst these summer trees
A sighing swaying seraph in the breeze

Thence splenetic things in seething spears of plunder
Split the skies in anvil chorus' of thunder
Smote Lorinda, cast her down
Her silent sweeps of tress caressed the ground
How her silent sweeps of tress caressed the ground

Envious summer skies in rancor put asunder
Us for loving one another; How I loved her
As my tear drops fell beside her, I knelt down in pangs and kissed her
In repose she lie forever
Wan Lorinda; Pale Lorinda, my sweet sister

With Another Man

What are the elements of time?
Incense burning in a cave deep dark and mystic
Night birds glowing even by day—turning things—unseen
The day brought on by some unseen candlewick
Gigantic in the sky

And why do things turn so?
Even things beautiful and so seemingly solid
Are they preordained because people change
If so, what if the heart grows pallid
(And begins to cry)

What if you've loved a woman for many years
And loved her, with passion and a deep tenderness
That goes to the roots of your heart and deeper
And you have expressed it with profound gentleness
In a word or a sigh

Yes, what if you've both changed a little and had misunderstandings
But things are reconcilable with effort
Because you're both very much like you always were
But its been blown out of proportion and you can't avert
Her passing though you try

And what, then, if she finds another man
And your paramount and mystic memories explode in a concussion
Upon the memory in a dream or an awakening
And you must face the fact its done
Though you cry and cry

On Sentiment & Understanding

There are times, of course, when too much emotion's wrong
When things are much the better left unsaid
We get our kicks through teasing or in pleasantry
Oh yes it adds such fun and such a repartee!

We yell and shout and slap another's shoulders
But don't get down to any deep emotion
In times of fun or festival affairs
It seems to me to be the best solution!

But there are times; there are times; that are real . . .
When exacting thoughtful phrases must be said
When we're tender and precise in what we feel
While we hit the nail clearly on the head

A friend is truly down and there's no kidding
That what he says is truly laced with pain
At times like this, we dearly need to bring
Our deepest thoughts to help our friends sustain

Our lovers robust ego has been pierced
A time to cast aside our meager strivings
And shun our own routine and get immersed
Totally into our lover while totally listening

The death of someone close is not a time
For shows of strength to offer someone near
There's a magnitude of love that is sublime
That is only given justice with our tears

The Wisdom Of Emotions

Yes, I have sometimes thought it's better
To make all my emotions level out
Being totally consistent to the letter
Never bothered or persuaded by the weather
Or lusty, down and out, or prone to shout

I tell myself beginning with the new year
I'll level out completely; always calm
I will keep myself unmoved and staid forever
And steady and from then on to endeavour
To make myself a vestibule of balm

But things begin to happen then
I'm seeing things not right or far too staid
I get angry, much too bored, and that is when
My emotions boil over, once again
Oh yes! And then I know of what I'm made!

I love to laugh and bluster and buffoon it
And even act the fool when it's right
To open up the atmosphere a bit
Occasionally I'll even be a wit
But all I want to do is bring on light!

And too, I cannot help but show my sadness
As long as I can listen just as well
To another's pain or sorrow, even gladness
For this planet is a paradox of madness
So we might as well express it to our fill

I Am A Speck To The Mountains

I can feel a trepidation
At the thought of standing tall
Where my shouts would bring reverberation
Because I might fall

Because too I'm a temporal being
Belonging to this life for but a while
When I'm gone the future people will be seeing
What projects from mundane flatness, often, a mile

I'll be obsolescent, yes, to earth
But the grand and mighty mountains will yet reign
Stupendously they'll usher in the birth
Of a billion other sunsets and sustain

Voluminous majestic and transcendant
Mountains of this planet loom on high
To be viewed by many and many an awed descendant
Will they see them as I as a tapestry to the sky?

Up serpentine tortuous trails ascending their heights
I have walked and have climbed to resuscitate self and soul
And sought to unveil their sinuous sleepy sights
To my mind and my psyche where tranquility is in toto

Everest Fuji McKinley the Materhorn all
Let me tarry not here at sea level I revere
What seem to demand that I answer their forlorn call
Negate them I won't though I feel an icy fear

The alpine prodigious dizzying lofty views
I acquire aspiring them grip me in fearful seizure
To fall I'd succumb to a heart attack and I muse
Climbing's adventure not leisure

But I'm rapt and imbibed with their grandeur and must go on
With my venturous predilection
To stay here and once not abscond
Would be dereliction

My life, aye, seems often so vague
So empty and fickle and lonely and full of rue
That I'll risk it as long as I'm sturdy enough and my legs
Can ascend to the wild blue

When it's spring in the mountains, the freshets pour down the canyons
I can watch from a mesa or ridge with attention above
With the igneous rock and the firmament my companions
And a thrill in my heart that enamours a man to love

I love how the mountains seem a dais for tall trees
And too how for lovers together, alone, they can make
A spiritual view in the background when romance sees
Their shadowy heights at a distance beyond a lake

And when twilight appears they are vivid against the sky
In my deference I am placid staid and still
As if in obeisance of body and muffled sigh
I appreciate God's great will

Although they inspire the doctrine of pantheism
Our Christian God only, salient and proficient
Could have sculpt them like that while a violent cataclysm
Would occur were there not this true God—so omniscient

I am a speck to the mountains
On Olympus do fountains of youth and love transpire
Flowing lazily on may my son taste of these fountains
And follow God's mountain's higher

Kenda

In his mind he can see her coming
Running just like the wind
And as fast as the wind
She is running

Somewhere there's a waterfalls on mars
Somewhere near a woman's singing softly
She is singing of her love
To the stars

All his life he has been so empty
And alone all the time
And it rings in his mind
He is lonely

Beauty is so common on her planet
But the men hold conceit
They are perfect; not sweet
She won't have it

All the women confirm he's ugly
They all call him a creep
Though he wants one to keep
One love only

And beauty is skin deep and so deceiving
No one on her planet understands her
Nobody thinks to care
While she's weeping

In his dream he can see it landing
When it ceases to roar
There is opened a door
She is standing

Somewhere there's a rocket ship ascending
Somewhere there's a woman born away
She's an outcast sent away
For not pretending

In her loveliness no one loves her
She has feelings too deep
For her planet to keep
They are cold there

One dark and lonely night when stars are dim
He hears a woman calling from the wasteland
She is holding out her hand
Meant for him

Through her eyes she can see him running
Running just like the wind
And as fast as the wind
He is coming

Somewhere there's waterfalls on mars
Somewhere there's a woman singing softly
She is singing with her love
To the stars

November

Chrysanthemums are living
The leaves bring bright topaz
All outdoors is shivering
Yet, offers what it has
In giving

Like forgotten dreams that flicker
Once again in late late fall
Disappearing even quicker
In heeding winters call
Is November

There is coldness far and near
The wistful self summation
Of this and other years
Sometimes brings dejections
And fears

But existence is a feather
For us all, not merely some
The chilling icy weather
Induces us to come
Together

October Wine

Remorse without reason atingles the spine
In the lonesome autumn months of the year
Yes things are getting sad for no reason
And the wind whips morose all the season
One wants October wine

Somnolent meadows are sober and calm
With occasional winds singing still
It's a vagabond wind to forestall
The winter preserving the fall
It's a vagabond wind to embalm

The perfect quintessence of autumn, it is
Compeer with September but late
Discerning the coldness to come
The breezes sing soft requiem
For the fall-obsequis

There's a hawthorne that's barren, alone in the wood
Poignant aloof and alone
Like the far away aerie in the skies
And the eagle that restlessly flies
Yes, flies! And if only I could

Enchantress! Enchantress! Entrapture me, fine
Oh dryad of bountiful love
Dissuade me from autumn's sad spell
Oh kiss me and bid me farewell
Oh fill me with lavender wine

Quandary

The dilemma of him deciding
What's best for his life is made slim
Or improbable and deriding
When she won't let him

She wields her love like the blinder
On a horse that is given direction
But her course is an ultimate binder
To his manly perfection

For she shuns all his aspiration
Does he hold her and forfeit his goals
Or feel love's deprivation
With a heart that's raked over the coals

The tragedy is, he loves her
And gives her an equal voice
But his spirit she tries to inter
Her love is his only choice

A steady appreaciation
And honour he heaps on her name
Yet, her emasculation
Could be his bane

And the irony is he's a man
Though she sees him but through her ego
Who'se effacing himself though he can
Make good of his skills something regal

The unfortunate choice is his own
She's made him the one to set free
His goals or to leave her alone
And that's the quandary

Courtesy

Why does it hurt
So much when another man
Fails to exert
A smile though he can
Or ignores us?

Because we love ourselves; it's true
We feel our existence
Is worth another's notice too
It hurts when his resistance
Brings pain

Why make the days go slower, still
(And a day can be so slow)
By adding to its toil the woe
Of a narrow-minded will
That brings hurt feelings?

The man who gives the common touch
And treats all men the same
Regarding small men just as much
Deserves a rightful claim
To blessedness

Enlightenment befalls to he
Who makes importance of
Those little acts of courtesy
A simple act of love
But so uplifting

Without that one ingredient
That humanizes us
We may reach the moon but our days are spent
Regrettably; it's useless
We've lived in vain

November Witch

Over the valleys, beneath the moon
Above a lovely lake
Fresher than clove and as blithe as the fields
Shimmeringly awake

Tis a keen kindred spirit and gentle of form
And her hair; it is kelp in the flowing
A statuesque and wonderful maiden-warm
And rich and knowing

The November witch! It is she
And the meads and the meadows adore her
Kindly and lovely and free
She hath travelled November, forever

A laurel wreath adorns her hair
She is deep as a cove but above
She is still but her heart she will share
Her diadem is love

And November winds come blowing across the fields
Whilst the pollen of flowers is tossed across the dell
But her champaign presence flits and soothes and heals
The aches of the heart and the spirit—very well.

Illustrious Sunday

Most of the time when I awake on Sunday
I foresee the day as listless melancholy and an effort to keep going
But this morning I awoke and knew some way
It would be different and the wind was boldly melodiously blowing

She was there, right away, with her smile
Her countenance was fresh and vital as the seashore
That we pursued early, hand in hand, for more than a mile
With our love erasing, nearly, the ocean's roar

We talked about where we were where we were going and what not
The important thing was that we were together
And able to realistically and romantically plot
Our future as lovers, in that weather

Before, we were as separate entities
Seldom planning anything at all as man and wife
But today we sheltered one another from the wind like lees
And heretofore, from that example, the winds of life

She entrusted me with some of her anxieties
I confronted her with mine and then a new consensus was begun
Our separate prides would be pushed aside for the priorities
Of our two emotions commingled into one

Thus our intimate joys could display through our lives
Reinforced by true love all the more
For the sand and sea roar to resound to the skies
When bonded and forming a shore

An emollient grace was given that way
From the comforting peace that we made
On our illustrious Sunday
We walked on as one unafraid

This Lady Of Pearl

Once my lady, slimmer and more supple, sat upon my hand, hers,
Adding all she had known, in divine captivity, ere I stole her
Of her charm, a pearl charm, an ancestral link,
Accrued to her, all in radiance, as a soft procession of quiescent maidens
Her grand family heritage

Satiny, her gown swept the aisle of our love
As it buffed my pearl better in each pulse throb
Of her descending steps

Mauve, her cheeks, paled purple
Shone in oozing light, still and faint, of mosaic paint
Glistening through, through the hue of the glass

Fragrant attar, sweet perfume of her, imbued me of clover
Redolent oceans partook of each pore even aerating more
Of a nearness persuasion not known even quite
In the bliss of her kiss before

Pulsatingly, I, reveled in the eyes of a loveliness born
Out of seaweed surrounded—unopened to me
On this day of all days
From her seashell like solitude

Floss streaming aspired in the March winds out there; Twas her hair
A chrysalis snatched from some far spreading tide,
Of an inlet firth, rolling in at her sides. How I
Mystified when I saw her afore had adored; Oh those eyes
Of whose venomous dearth seared the breadth and the depth
Of my psyche whilst I'd sighed at her

Now, she flowed with her hair in the churchyard out there, divine
On this day of her vow of all time

Grey Faces

To another town—far far away—I travelled
I settled in a dark and lonely bar
I saw so many old and shadowed faces
And when I left it lingered and the traces
Of those faces when I got back in the car
Its effect on me unraveled

Those faces seemed so void and oh so nameless
They indeed were very tired and so old
The situation made me feel the same
Like a lost and lonely man without a name
In that distant bar I felt so cold
Apart and even useless

The words they spoke were pattered like the raindrops
That fell into a forest dim and cold
Held back by giant trees until they sprinkle
In intermittent drops and slowly spill
On a dark and shadowed forest floor so old
Where the shadows never stop

For their words were low—so low and yes, so muffled
Not spirited at all, and yes, so void
Brought down by years of sorrow waste or apathy
And when I left it lingered, I was ruffled
With a feeling that I usually avoid
Would those faces ever be me?

Erotica

In the dim morning light she can stimulate
The id of the daylight all around
Suppressing its power to emulate
Its focus she moves without sound
And her wit is ambiquous
But her body contiquous

Mirrored is her form in the bureau, there
The breezes of morning breathe soft
Her nakedness stirs with her golden hair
She leans and her form is aloft
So directly in front of me
This heart drums to ecstasy.

Her features are classic, she teases me
With a subtle ambiquous wit
But warm is her attitude-warm yet free
It seems she will please quite a bit

But the question is, when will she?
I am thinking, oh, fervently!

I am thinking, oh, fervidly!

Warm is her substance, oh soundly warm!
Aware with a sweet empathy
She moves and her parts are a loving swarm
And she gazes now coy down on me
But my needs she has knowledge of
And her vessel is fraught with love

I'm exploding, she bends and but touches me
But then she explodes, kissing full
Our bodies are pounding in rhapsody
I summon her softly and pull
Her into the bed with me
And I touch her so gently

We stroke with our words and our loving hands
We know one another's sweet souls
The tantalized trip is to foreign lands
While my sabre imperically grows
To thrust and to conquer her
She'll conquer me too! (It's sure!)

Were exploding the trip had been slow till now!
Exploring so sweetly and soft
But my God! She's destroying me, driving foul
All thought and my mind is aloft!
She's shrieking and I am too
Oh my God!! Oh my God!!! Oh God!!!!!!!!!!!!

Melinda

I was imaginative but not so wild
As was she whose whole outlook seemed a vagary
Melinda roamed as a restless child
Too transient and fancy free

I admit that I tried to copy
Her whimsical ways for a while
In hopes she'd discover she loved me
But I wasn't her style

I wanted life's better things too
Yet, she saw it a commoner's quirk
That I visioned her wonderful castle
Would be made of hard work

The thing that hurt most was the brain
Of this brilliant young woman began
To view me with utter disdain
As a simple hard working man

I poured out my feelings but she
Never heard and talked only of herself
As if I had no personality
Putting me on the shelf

For I learned I was just a receptacle
An experimental toy
For her sizeable flagrant ego
She considered me just a boy

Now, another love I have found
Who'se imaginative, also true
And has both her feet on the ground
Melinda, she isn't like you

This woman is tender and real
She thinks I'm a prince of a man
And I'll get her that castle, I feel
Melinda, I'll show you I can

Senora The Spirit

The clouds; they are dark clouds, they fill the sky
They are ink purple clouds in the sunset
They fill the wanderer, he, who travels on
He who travels the night and beyond
Behold! Behold the spirit God with a start; a sigh
The thought is Senora, Senora

The night is a cavern of brindled ink
A sensation of loneliness throbbing
To seize the traveler, he, who travels here
In his throbbing insatiable fear
Behold, behold the traveler! Her sweet caress
Was visioned by him, T'was Senora!

The clouds; they are perfume; they fill the night
They are somnolent clouds kissing softly
To soothe the wayfarer, he, who sings aloft
In a realm of her charms sweet and soft!
Behold! Behold! Vision the tenderness
Imagine Senora! Senora!

Apostrophe To Love

Venerable sylph, terrestrial being
Edify verity candor and seeing
Of love and of rapture of sweet vinous things
Sprite tell me more of mellifluous flings

Satiate finely sweet vernal sweet schemes
Surreptitious longings and unbounded dreams
Enchantment adoring; Why vagary be?
Press on eternal propinquity!

Expedite ardor. Perspicacious seeming;
Stellar melodious, august deeming

Palatial wisteria; Unfurled climbs
Embellish beatitude obelisk rymns
Acclaim like a paean's intrinsic grace
Love's lyrical essence of fond embrace

Limp languor made nebulous passions profound
Redeeming in true love loyalty bound

Spire, superscribe no love a taciturn thing
Mix nought of a visage of love's quiet spring
Supersede virulent vapid lives
Stress love from which nurture derives

The Cat

A stealthy quiet creature cool and sane
It's shrouded much in mystery and darkness
We love it for its quietude, the same
In a world nearly venomous with frankness

The eyes can say it purely when we touch
And stroke the pulseful carpet of its fur
And gratitude is given very much
In the huskiness of its purrs

What wisdoms never I
Will know does it possess
There is poignancy in each eye
That sometimes makes me shudder; I confess

In the night amidst the silence
It seems to turn my thoughts within its brain
With a look of near defiance
Even adamant disdain

The centures I see upon its brow!
There's regal atavism in its bearing
The ancient streets of Crete once saws it prowl
In that night time long remote were two eyes glaring

I sense a quiet dignity
A look within its eyes
That urges love so warmly
It can't disguise

When it's warm and near
Its look seems not a bane
So solemn and sincere
How could it feign?

To That Lake Of My Youth

Its shoreline shared the loneliness
Of a young boy in his wandering;
And indeed its length brought peacefulness
From the world surrounding,
Enveloping him.

Its waters rippled
With a gentleness that brought peace to console
And the sound of a young bird crippled
(Moved detachment from his soul.)
It taught him love.

And here he was monarch.
He could feel importance.
When after came his friend, the dark
Erasing all pangs of discordance,
He was at ease.

Amid the wind which whipped his back and shivered,
The little man stepped lightly along the lakeside
From his fears and was delivered
For, yes, he could confide
In the lake.

That lake was a source of enchantment
But it was more. He could get away
From his young anxieties that plagued him and seemed scant
To his loved ones but were real to him in a great way.
(Thoughts too much for his mind.)

Here, the bullfrog's croak and twilight's hue
Took him into another world.
Low faint animal sounds and a watery view
Left his heart at last unfurled.
He was himself.

The perfection of the lullabies
From the night birds which arose
With a flutter to the shadowy skies
Made him think to, here, repose
Beside the lake.

And so, only then, did he feel
The need to go back whence he came
From that solitude meant to heal,
Leaving him not the same.
Yes, I walked home.

Lyrical & Lovely Thoughts

The seashore at twilight—a woman holding
Your hand—swaying sweetly with the sea breeze
Saying sweetly that she loves you—and other
Things

An acknowledgement and giving
A reaching out—being touched
With love—and touching
Back

Rich imagination with the twilight
Expressive lofty love for those
You live for—showing it
Intensely

All the time and with the dawn and
In between, yes,—all the time
With fervid power or!
(Gentleness)

Lofty deed and lofty word and thought
Sprinkled with imagination's charm
Running through the forest holding hands
Charmed

Loving on the ocean's crashing shore
Kiss your lover's lips while she's asleep
Awaken with a passion—and a look
Sparkling

Unoccasioned presents, cards, and words
Catching unaware a lover's heart
Inventions of abandon—spontaneity
Given

Winter Dream

'Tis as cold as the night she passed.
The snow; it has covered the evergreens.
How many long years have elapsed
Since they discovered such winter scenes?

The valley is chilly and white.
The footpath he's taking is sinuous.
The snow has been falling all night,
Making his journey more perilous.

And the fences and barn need mending
And the kine must be fed in the morn;
Though his body is hard at bending
For he's tired and old and worn.

But he's climbing the timeworn valley,
Imagining of that day
They walked up the path in ecstasy
And paused at its summit to pray.

He remembers her way of blushing
In the cold and the crisp winter air.
How the blood of his heart came rushing
When he kissed her and held her near.

All fear was erased in knowing
That she loved him and him alone.
Her breathtaking smile kept glowing
Through tempests and storms that had blown.

And his thoughts are more deep than the valley
And his heart is as pure as the snows.
He’s content with the rush of her memory,
Quickening as he goes.

Enchantra— Lady Sleep

DIANA, Dear Diana,—mystic maiden of the moon
Do you have a beauteous daughter?
Does she make me fall asleep soon?
In my fortress of the night
(I've often sought her)

I have wandered many gloamings
In a life time filled with pain
She has comforted all my roaming
She has shielded me from the rain

The chilling rains neath staid nocturnal starlight
The winds that came in rancor
Terrible in the night!
(And in my languor)

Sweet Diana, She is lovely
She's a silken sylph. Her tress
Perfumes and enthralls me
So I feel my burdens less
(My psyche is free)

Aurevoir, my hurt and suffering
I was indisposed till now
To face the torment life can bring
To sink within its' slough

Her tender charms will bring me peace
And spiritually allay
All diurnal thoughts, like geese
Shall fly away

Incipient sleep will hold
Me tenderly
Till nocturnal arms enfold
My soul, completely

Ah, that is Enchantra,
Lady Sleep. I know it when
In dreams I smell the flora
(Of she who soothes as none can)

One Love For Me

Always in spring I remember
At hours near dawn
One who'se passed forever
Her spirit is gone

But I feel among a host of tears
Trodding this earth in May
That never the days and the death and the years
Shall quite ever take her away

Sure, my psyche is sometimes sad
But my woman was something good
She was special and something I had
Back in time when I fully understood

The gentleness passion and thoughtfulness of
(Romance intertwined by need)
Concern and the fervor of love
Will ne'er in my heart recede

And I cannot bring memory back
Through another the mist of my mind
Blocks loneliness always I lack
Nothing; she was one of a kind

Chauntaclear

His name was Von and he came upon
A horse of shining stature.
He was debonair with an essence rare
And he'd galloped all the way from Chauntaclear.

He sought a bride in his wild ride
To belong to him forever,
Who would ride with him to the sunset dim
And accompany him to Chauntaclear.

He was tall and dark with a regal mark.
It was many many years since he came here
On a virile steed of a noble breed
That was bred in the realm of Chauntaclear.

When he arrived not a girl survived
To parry his sweet demeanor.
He was strong of arm and full of charm
And developed his aplomb in Chauntaclear.

And the thought arose and the question posed
To make the issue clearer:
Would he refuse or would he choose
A love to betroth in Chauntaclear?

And how they schemed and how they beamed
When he came into view or nearer!
Aye, they fiercely fought and with vengeance sought
This gallant young man from Chauntaclear.

Lo, quite by chance Von looked askance
And spotted a girl dearer
To his heart and home he had ever known
In his wayward attempts from Chauntaclear.

She was rather plain but was cool and sane
And she set his heart afire.
For her soul was pure and her presence dear.
He imagined her home in Chauntaclear.

Her name was Ann. She had known no man
To parley affection for her,
But he wrote her verse, "Twas intense and terse,
And regaled her with tales of Chauntaclear.

And he held her tight while they rode one night
Into their fiery future,
With a happy cry and in each a sigh,
All the way to Chauntaclear.

The Park

Twilight comes down on the summer scene
Lackadaisical like a leaf, but unlike the children
On those far reaching carpets of green
Where they run

The arc of a softball is lessening
Like moments that fade all away
The sounds and the laughter are spring
And the children play

Somewhere off in a cold cold cavern
Reverberating; a heart
Echoing only the stern
Detached from the scene and apart

Where fresher meadows and moments from another twilight
Rest lies its essence; but memory
Here, a shadow of itself, no more bright
And nevermore, free

The filtering laughter from all around
The strolling of lovers the children
Suspend and are muffled by sights and sounds
Of a time when two sweethearts were one

The day that was perfect has gone away
The love that was perfect has died
Perfection comes once; "Twas a passing day
His cold heart aspires—to cry

The Sweetest Summer Hour

[In All Memory]

Lotuses of divine loveliness lingering in lakes outstretched for miles,
Placid are the lakes, skies and meadows of this day
Committed to memory and mainly its finest hour
When the wide circle of humanity is lessened to a circumference of smiles.

The circle of difference retains its difference, yes,
So identity keeps identity and doesn't forsake that
But the distance around is lessened to give empathy.
Everywhere people join hands in a sunshine of tenderness.

There is a strong scent of spring and summer,
Commingled together in a kaleidoscopic aroma of green meadows,
Outreaching to the mind, heart and eye with a feeling of togetherness,
So gloriously sweet as to seemingly last forever!

No man fears holding back his heart, if his thoughts are grand.
And all thoughts are on this day; this incredible hour
When the human heart has reached its finest pinnacle
And every man rejoices at the positives of every other man!

Oh, I can see them recite with fluent flair their appreciation
Of their differences,
Acknowledging one another as separate but wonderful entities!
The circle is never made into a line for the identity would be gone,
But there is love reverberating around that circumference!

And the women are gloriously, magnificently radiant!
All like maidens who revere their men, singing sweetly,
For they are all regarded as queens by the gallant men,
Where love and respect and adoration are concerned; there is no
want!

And the meadows and the air and the people of this hour
Are perfumed by a perfume and a feeling that cause poetic words.
It flows from their golden throats resplendent with wine like
Phrases

Till everyone is drunk with love's herculean power!

Each Precious Moment

There is a quality about all things
That makes them singular and precious
Every moment that life brings
Should not be minimized by us.

To look out into an autumn haze
And see the particular cloud pattern
And how each leaf falls and lays
Is to make the spirit burn.

Somewhere there are children playing
Under the bright corona of the moon
Some have grown whose lives are graying
We get older too soon.

And no day or moment will ever
Return amid its good or bad
Once gone, it is lost forever
And I find this unspeakably sad.

Madeline

In an orchard or by the sea
Madeline waits for me
She is the goddess of my dreams
The forbidden woman of my schemes
Those idle schemes of passions swept
From in me burning where they're kept
When the nightfall's visionary
Dreams bring on imaginary
Scenes of Madeline

In the desert by the nile
Distant lands I trek a while
Arabs passing wear their turbans
I am drunk of ale and bourbons
With the beauty of this creature
Tempting me I try to reach her
Soon because my dream shall pass
The shapelier than an hourglass
Lurid Madeline

Be this dream scenario?
There I view a gay kimono
I have come to the land of flowers
Geisha girls shrines and towers
Cherry blossoms by the million
Where stands proud the gold pavilion
Madeline in the cherry dance?
Much I marvel, in a trance
Sensuous Madeline

Kaleidoscopic with out reason
Is my dream a different season
Turns amid Victoria falls
Madeline on its summit calls
Breathlessly the scene yet changes
African planes my spirit ranges
Antelope bound and pass me by
Kilimanjaro looms on high!
Where is Madeline?

Lo! Behold a windswept station
Here I feel a cold sensation
White robed lands of polar bears
Madeline in my nearness dares?
Running flowing to entice
Me across this snow and ice
Of a sudden warm are chill sleets
White bleak regions are my bedsheets
Gone is Madeline!

Encomium To The Wind

It's melody is that of a wise old god
Sweeping majestically or quietly forlorn
Who as a mortal might have trod
Some ancient time in human form

Intense or softly tranquil
With gentle wafts or rushes where
Evolves a tremulous trill
Crescendo sounds in air

Aloft atop the mountain climes
Where the condor sits or sails
Absconding away many times
Riding the winds to the dales

The winds that reign oer the cryptic night
Withal as the condor's search
Which whine in his treacherous flight
To a precipice aerie's perch

Summoning some; it asks that they wander
Miles and miles from home
Winds melancholy then cause them to ponder
Making moot their yearnings to roam

Sensing trouble hobeit one goes
In his whirlwind venturesome quest
Discerning the violent squalls
Of this life that is fickle at best

There are battlefields quiet at last
Where the whimpering winds knell the toll
Of soldiers long dead from the past
Sad and mournful they restlessly blow

Like a requiem music so sad
Saith the wind, why must needlessly flow
Their life blood they're never that bad
Tell me what; tell me what does it show

But the flowers bloom always again
And the wind moves their sepals in the rain
Caressing their calyxes, too, when they wane
A lover of nature a swain

For in wisdom one knows that all things
Are destined to pass though they're grand
And the wind in a lilt often sings
The glory of god through the land

Perse, all alone, through all time
Interminable time it has howled
An esprit through the ages sublime
Interspersing in glee and loud

When Neanderthal man walked the ground
Let's regress to that ancient day dim
The windy tumultuous sound
Made his warn cavern hearth allay him

And revive all his spirit the pith
Of the winds when he sought fresh quarry
Roaming his olden age with
The gales of an estuary

The wind who inspired vast legions to vanquish
Taking Caesar's footsoldiers abroad
In to alien lands till they tired to languish
Weary for Roman sod

The intermittent winds benign
Bringing home the palmer
Sleepy in his homeward pine
Somnolent and calmer

From a hill that in Jerusalem
Jesus taught up high on
Exalting to Elysium
The holy hill of Zion

And the venerable wind was there
To resuscitate Jesus' soul
Like a seraph in the air
While a palmer played the oboe

To reminisce and ponder things
From the abyss of time ago
Quixotic thoughts of castles or kings
Is to hear the wild wind blow

On Poseidon's seas to ancient Greece
To Olympus where gods once strode
Seeking worldly peace or golden fleece
From they're mythical yore abode

Pellucid to our present age
A potentate of the land
A mystic intangible sage
Who'se omnipresent hand

Can carry us to Samoa
A hermes transporting our souls
To listen we hear an aloha
Or feel the lonely shoals

Of vagabond rivers like the Thames
The Seine or the Rhine or the Nile
To places with far away names
Like Valparaiso in Chile

One senses Jamaica winds
Or Java winds and ocean gales
The froth from the waters rescinds
Beneath the schooner's sails

And how peaceful is a loch
The wind adores
Whispering under a dock
Watching the shores

Singing lovely lullabies
Sonorous to a roar
Morose as a waif who cries
Somber oer a moor

No doldrums go where breezes flow
Virile on a trail ride
Through steep plateau that's pastoral
Beautiful high and wide
Where wonderful breezes glide
Like a marvelous blushing bride
And ephemeral eddys
Tossle there
The hair and unsteady
A pompous air

But that redolent mesa breeze
Becalms the wanderer's fear
The verdure he smells and sees
Renders his heart secure

And it renders us all; the wind
In one way or another
Perhaps he's our next of kin
Inspiriting us forever

The Season

In December I am certain
Brisk snowflakes made a curtain.
How swiftly did they beckon
Two spirits in to one.

For as we touched in winter
A wraith of wind blew o'er
Two hearts betide in rapture.
A staid wind blew no more.

Somber wafts had whisked in autumn
Sad and wistful, softly spoken,
Lo, my psyche bemoaned that season
'Twas my heart a barren moor,

Till I chanced upon this maiden.
Oh, how softly did she beckon
And we paused beneath an aspen
As we passed along the shore

While the zephyr moved the aspen,
Sodden snowflakes fell forgotten
We were rapt as if in heaven,
As I held her-under there.

Siren of the lake

Viva the night, funereal and vague
To match uncertainties that inundate my mind
Yet, in its quietness it soothes the thoughts that plague
I have tried to leave behind

Serene and soothing are their hold
The beatific murmur of the breezes
That along the lake unfold
A woman seems the wind that willfully teases

'Neath quicksilver stars the somnolent aroma
Of the junipers is tonic for my psyche
Very vivid is the moon and her corona
With a clarity and. luster that I like

Where magnolias and cypresses abound
I view the lake
And leave them for the shoreline little sound
Do I make

A drumming is my heart's pulsation inside
Stirred by quiet that's extreme
With the darkness far and wide
And the insect legions teem

A visual abeyance is my scan
For to see what might be near
Deep in darkness where no man
Has walked but me brings quivering and fear

And a stupefaction's covering me
I gaze upon the waters as entranced
With a memory of whiskey
That' s left my sad demeanor unenhanced

Though my vision is acute
I cannot see with clarity
And in emptiness I'm mute
My spirits into atrophy entirely

Like the waters caught in stillness
I am taciturn and torpid while immersed
In my spirit's awful illness
And the throe of broken love that's not dispersed

Through my nebulous thoughts is heard a grackle's call
In ascent from out the thickets to the night
It confirms this lonely pall
So singular and distant is it's flight

Grim and wistful I imagine
I can vision any thought or sense of smell
Is that why that I now fashion
In my mind the smell of perfume, who can tell?

Exuding from thin air a pleasant waft
Of the sweet allaying fragrance is enthralling
And discerning its aroma, am I daft?
Lord, I fathom I can hear a woman calling!

It's an intonation calling me without
An inhibition honeyed with desire
Reassuring me and do I hear about
A mandolin a viol, and the lyre?

I find myself exploring 'neath the stars
The sounds are more sonorous, Lord I see
A woman from the moon or maybe Mars
Who is holding out her arms outstretched to me!

And in groping in my haste and swift pursuance
I care not if she's real, she is pure
Be she tangible or alcohol's influence
Through these breezes she can comfort me, It's clear

Very ravishing is she, her green eyes glow
Her bluish hairs alluring and she's svelte
Accosting her my heart doth quickly know
'Tis the brightest fire of love I've ever felt

Time Passes — And Is Gone

Time passes and time is gone
Like an evanescent leaf the wind has blown,
Leaving trepidations that a new dawn
May one day come and find us so alone,

I've scented time when Autumn's in the air,
I've seen it in the children passing on.
In dreams of falling darkness it is there
To be with us a moment, then abscond.

The luster and the radiance of her
Will never fade away as long as I
Have a heart; were it to live forever
The love in it for her would still not die.

And many years from now when she is gray.
I'll grasp her precious love and say that I'm
In love in such a deep resplendent way,
Immeasurably profound*untouched by time.

Time passes and is gone
Like obsolescent leaves the wind has blown.
Together we will touch the distant dawn.
Living it together-not alone.

Autumn Years

In our Autumn years, darling, when
Thoughts of love that come again
Tumble out from our hearts' source
When as before; They run the course
Of happy thoughts; Two memories one
My darling come

Into my presence and my heart
As from the start

Of our courtship's young romance
Our nostalgia may enhance
What was once a love so new
Me and you

And when ourselves grow old and grey
We'll stirringly court again this way
Among the pines
Our tender wines
Will show us then

Of a love that once had been
In our springtime, darling, and when
The Autumn's chill
Our hearts will fill
(Once again)

The Shoreline At Sunset

No drunk in his sweetest abandon
Could fall with the grace of those waves
They fall upon my heart amid the night
Then ebb with utter beauty out again

The night enshrouds it's moorings
I hear some distant ship
How lonely is a ship far out at sea
While the surf comes smashing in

The shoreline rich in resonance
Accents the torrid beauty of the skies
The cloud patterns are beautiful
A shock of different shades amid the dusk

When the tide disperses slowly
It's memories receding in the mind
That shriek back their reality
When the breakers pound the shore

Memories of faces
And a million different moments in a life
Are scattered on the shoreline
Sweetly strewn or filled with pain

All the recollections move a man
And hold while gentle waters ripple in
There are images within them
Particular to him

Her Love

The sweetest moments
Of the finest summer day
Of the grandest year in all eternity,
That is what she's given me
That is her love.

Like the purest fragrance
From a loving flower
In it's finest hour
I have ever known
It's this to me.

No woman is or was
In all eternity
An equal to the love
That she has given me
There's no one, no.

Like the dearest memory
Of a river wine
That flows forever,
Lost In time
Her kiss,

And the greenest meadows
And the softest streams
With gentle pleasures
And golden dreams
(Her Love)

To a Drunkard – Humor

Dreadful! You're floundering here
And how your head must bang
Murmuring, sickened from beer
You give my heart a pang

Dear God! What is the fault
Of outcasts born to suffer
That they must abscond to the malt
When stormier lives get rougher

Penitence! Can't they find it in church
As compeer then with you and I?
Or crestfallen, do they feel their smirch
(Is not forgiven in mankind's eye)

Truly, Yes, Truly it's wrong
Undertaking to sanctify
Just the lofty till he can't belong
He wants to die!

Beseeching! I beg for you, sir!
Think back to a time when you sang
Of a sweet life much happier
When your head didn't clang-

Stormy seas, Lo
They have taken you down
Your conscious is full of woe
There you lie on the ground

But arise now and suffer no more
Feel the balm of my love; I know
There's a happier shore
Where the true waters flow

Little Girl

Before have I never inquired
Why you have oft walked this way?
Only because I'm inspired
By someone I'm asking today

Do you have thoughts surreptitious
That one day he might take your hand?
Radiant thoughts so delicious
Of one who will think you are grand

Have you imagined of dancing
With him out under the stars?
A slow minuet that's entrancing
Taking you yonder to mars

But maybe you're yet, just a girl
With sidewalks and jacks in your mind
Still in an innocent swirl
Don't leave it too soon behind

The reason you find me so curious
Is that you remind me of her
When she was young and as precious
Back in that distant year

Thinking how much she is cherished
I'm saddened considering this
Some little girls have perished
Before they have ever been kissed

Please take good care little princess
So someday you'll feel as she
A glowing voluptuous Mrs.
In love with some fellow like me

Now, maybe it's just incidental
That your passing my way, It's true
Forgive me I'm sentimental
And today I'll be saying—I do

Time Traveler

Will you come with me in my time machine;
And we will scan the ages
I'll show you how we'll set things straight
We'll' turn back histories' pages

Naphtha planets will glimmer and glow
We'll shatter through a shimmery flow of stars
I will decipher the milky way
And you will take nectar from Mars
We shall offer the nectar to Jupiter
An oracle will be ours
Our Oracle will overcome the pathos of the ages
Our treatise obtained of the mightiest sages

We'll follow the paths of the heavens from nadir
By way of the nova night
Many an opal mercury moon will guide us aright

On On to this carnage of super stars
They who have guided mankind
We will alter their offal and leave them behind

The light Through The Window

The night light of telephone poles
The neighbor's windows and perhaps the moon
Filters through the curtains of our room
So dark amid my wife's sleeping
And my lying here, alone
While this spirit tells me
What it knows

Our children sleeping
Like cheerful little candles
Gone out for the moment
Remind me in my mind
That I was once, like them
Looking out through other windows
(My spirit's weeping)

For since that day
The windows have changed
I have seen many windows
And broader horizons
But seldom the love
They had for me
As a "boy

The message is this
The window of this bedroom
With it's light in the dark
Is a connecting link
To my window as a boy
And the true loves I've known
(Are but them and her bliss)

My Patriarch, The Night!

Oh breezes of the deep nocturnal void!
Oh offer me your cathedral tune!
Like those stately domes that lift above the town
Oh this patriarch, the night, it is so deep
And so sublime!

The majestic rains that fall upon the town
Oh the thunder and the lightning coming down
I can sense it's depth and sense it's royal power
Can't you sense it's sensitivity and power!
Oh late night hour!

The night, it sits in splendor and aplomb
Like a potentate of time serene and calm
I appreciate your sight!
Oh wise majestic night!
I revel within your calmness or your might!

The eternity of time is in your portals
Yes, I sense the things you've seen and taken in
Could I walk with you and travel through your gates
While enveloped in your darkness, some time late
I am sure I'd taste the wisdoms of the fates!

Oh late night hour, oh late night hour; oh late
There's the calmness of infinity to date
You are patient; you are wise
You have tasted all of time
And the airy currents and shadows are your eyes

(And somehow you understand, oh night)
For your quiet wisdom beckons us to think
And to be much more serene and introspective
To be fairer, more forgiving, and more calm
(And more reflective)

The Twilight At the End of Day

The twilight at the end of day
Faint and low
In a very unusual way
Renews my soul

On the horizon there is a tint
There is a dimming light
And it gives precursor hints
Of the coming night

If I happen to be outdoors
A summary of my life
Projects from my memories stores
I miss my wife

I have been out there
On a golf course at twilight's beginning
And visoned her hair in the air
Was what caused the shimmering

In the faltering day a hiatus
Breaks thoughts of the game and I find
I must sum up the day from a syllabus
Quiet discourse through my :mind

And more faintly still fades the sun
I'm a pensive man at this hour
Once, alone, when the night had begun
The world seemed dour

Yes, it used to be more the severe
Before I found love and was wed
Now, the knowledge she'll soon be near
Clears loneliness from my head

And really I'm renovated
For I've put all my cares on the wing
And the solitude I once hated
Is a passing thing

A Delicate Balance

I believe a life
Is like a pendulum
And It swings and swings
From joy and then to strife
And back again where It started from
Ay, it brings
Discrepancies

I believe a man
Is tender certainly
Though he'll climb and climb
To do all that he can
Devoid of love he can easily
In some time
Disintegrate

I believe we must
In earnest compensate
For when fortunes veer
By placing all our trust
In someone's heart who we designate
To cohere
Devotedly

I believe the more
That life's precarious
But it can be won
When we in faith outpour
Our love that brightens the whole of us
Like the sun
Decidedly

What I Want To Do

I want to gather those moments
So precious for recalling in my brain
So sweet upon my soul I feel a pang
Divulging what has "been

I want to gather their substance
And put them in a jar to ever remain
The sweetest songs of" life that I have sung
That I can never live again

The way the morn seemed once
The way I ran through forests in the rain
Through cobwebs thrilled and shrieking at the bang
Of the thunder and the dew drops, I was ten

I want to hold to my bosom
My loves that were not love so long ago
Infatuation never meant to last
Attingled me and made me feel alive

The ones I thought I loved who thought me dumb
The memory fresh and tender seems to glow
To think I was so carefree in that past
It's grand to feel in love when ten and five

Those long awaited days that had to come
But seemed to come so infinitely slow
Now, I think they surely come too fast
Graduation ne'er will be revived

But the dearest and the tenderest by far
Of the memories beloved to my soul
Is my courtship; oh my lord; I. cannot say
The profundity she's given; never, no!

Like a precious tiny loving little star
In a universe of black and lonely coal
She has loved me oh so deeply to this day
'Twas god who beat the odds my heart doth know

For this sagely kind and omnipresent czar
Led me to her heart from out the shoal
And a myriad of days so dark and grey
Oh my lord! Oh dearest god! I love her so!

Despair

Despair is when one's hope and pride
Have sought and struggled side by side
And lost in agony—and died
And it's grievously hard to stand aside
And let them pass if one has tried
Especially and I confide
If one has held them long and vied
For something better

It follows then and I contend
That one must not despise a friend
Who falls because his heart won't mend
From bitter fate he could not fend
Who hates to follow such a trend
But cannot help it in the end
If once that heart would miles distend
(That heart that now feels hopeless)

The Heat Of A Summer Day

Life's worth seems debatable
On a day like this; the sidewalks
irradiate summer, unbearable
In the heat and a feeling in my throat
Like chalk

While I cross the town, my deterrent
Is the sickening question that why
Is there so much hate apparent
And violence in the world and callousness
I sigh

And yet there is the heat; always
The heat that seems unmoved
Impassive in it's rule over my days
Perhaps there's many people with a heart
Unproved

The beatings; the senselessness
The somber cold unfeeling of so many
The selfishness; the thoughtlessness
I ask myself this question about love
Is there any?

And does it all tie in?
Is this heat a stern extension of the people
In their rash and noisy din
Without quality and meaning seems the day
An inferno

Can any person see me as I stroll
These streets for whatever destination
And feel me in them and truly know
The feelings that I have through this veil
Of perspiration

If we'd strengthen everybody that we meet
And understand with friendliness and ardor
The sun would seem a warm and glorious heat
Stunning us with torrents full of love
And splendor

Lord, I know we must look at others
Not with ego. But in a fashion
That our hearts can be another's
And we must look. We must look
With compassion

He Said To Me

Grandpa dear
I asked him
Why haven't you married again?
Her cerements have all wasted
Why dwell on what has been?

He looked on me with a sadness
I then could not understand
A fathomless tired sadness
And held me with one hand
And answered yes

But her eyes were bluer, son
Than misty morning skies
Yes, they were the bluest, son
That I have ever seen
(And they were the truest)

Her maiden curls so long ago
Of our restless fall
Perfumed me when I was near
She was the grandest I ever saw
(She was the grandest I ever saw)

The Difference in People

Behold! the day! it's nuances and charm
The heat can be rigid as a gendarme
And the people who walk it forever
Can be rigid or cruel or clever

Take notice the sun in the heavens!
It shines on the tumult of persons
And sometimes I wonder just why
When they pass without batting an eye

Hooray for the mean summer weather
Inflexibly tougher than leather
And the people who are just the same
Opinionated and tough they remain

I cannot relate to the summer
When the heat and the sun and the bother
Seems much like some people
(Unyielding; inflexible)

But the night in it's deepening fog
Seems to offer a dialogue
It touches my heart with it's mildness
Like someone who listens in quietness

And people are different too
Some give of themselves to you
So mild so sweet and so tender
With hearts that will yield and bend there

There are those who but smother and shove
But some who will listen with love
They bend but are stronger
They talk but they hear

Her Secret

Some tantalize—sly—with a flickering eye
These women of foxy demeanor
Running off like a jet; they play so hard to get
And are tougher to catch than a whisper

(That's because they're loyalties not nearly)
As touching and as tender as is hers
So naturally with words of love she came to me
In our love's first timeless hours

And that memory will ever more be deeper to me
Than a man's who has had to compete
When his lady's too free and cannot quite agree
Who to pick from the lovers she greets

She was never like this; my beloved miss
From the start, it was me; me alone
And her breathtaking kiss with it's innocent bliss
Was the purest and dearest I've known

Loyalty and tender words of love to me
Is the secret that sets her apart
Loving warmly with discriminate fidelity
Is her secret that has overflowed my heart

Night Leaves

I have felt them
Falling down at various times. in my existence^
Broken from their stems
By the wind's insistence.

In a pirouette they crinkle on my heart
Or rather the ground
That' s moist and damp in the night and they dart
With nary a sound

They fall on my heart so much
I cannot rake them away
When melancholy thoughts have such
A mood of grey.

But the night I met my one true love
They were kindred spirits in air
In our stroll through the park how they fell from above.
Ah yes I first kissed her there.

However I've often been bleak
Here upon while I've forged with my soul
Through problems in life and I seek
Some identity this I know

I have wrangled and wrestled and fought
To forget all the woes that have been'
But when I am overwrought
I fall down in spirit again.

And then with the starlight I walk
To. think, till my judgment believes
I'll somehow suffice as I stalk
Through the night leaves.

Animal Heaven

Is there somewhere far away
In the far away sky
Where animals go to stay
When they die?

Some distant shadowy region not
Forgotten by god's grace, there
Where animals we loved a lot
Go because we care

A place devoid of hate
And cruelty
Where no one can abate
Or hurt in glee

A mist so fine must curl, here
A warming mist that warms
Where silvery starlight shimmering peers
Upon the animals forms

On this night land ever dark
Animals shadowy go
A blissful purr or a happy bark
Follows the cool wind's flow

All happiness reigns high
No hurt, It's understood
Not scorned in life by loving eyes
There were those eyes that would

Away upon some distant swan
Ascend my thoughts and they are gone
Where foggy dreams and misty realms
Becalm amid some shady elms.

The shadows of my brindled heart
Are pacified and made apart
Here, love at last no fancy flight
Is elevated in it's night.

And too my lofty sweetest thought
Is garnered by some angel, not
Detached, she's reassuring me
With honeyed words of rhapsody.

No star is greater than our will,
No more the wind's disdainful chill
That shrieked upon my heart, a shroud;
It's emptiness is disavowed.

The wind becomes a lullaby,
The pith of it. is but a sigh;
And viewing of the earth from here
I see the meadows far and near.

And rills that flow upon my mind
Are mingled with this angel's wine
Whose aromatic essence flows
And sweetens me, my spirit glows.

The night, no more a foghorn shrill
Of murkiness upon my will,
Is but a woven tapestry
Of stars that bind her love for me.

I love her too because she cares
As I for her; her spirit dares
To know and understand my mind,
Acknowledging with words so kind.

Reality would think it wrong
To lift another's heart to song,
Suspending with serenity,
Incessant with amenity.

I feel grand tranquility
Descending now intrepidly,
For what's imagined can be real,
Out of time or space, I feel.

Marissa

Marissa, was a storm
That blew through my life and flew
Away in the night her warm.
Earnestness soothed me too

Bringing her deep concern
She blew me the breath of pride
I had of myself to learn
When she stayed at my side

To her I was no stepping stone
But someone to admire
And she did and attempted to hone
Into me yet more fire

She wasn't in love I knew
But made me feel worthwhile
Warmth was within her. I grew
In love of life a mile

And too I did not love her
Yet gave of my own guiding hand
She gazed in my eyes with wonder
And I felt grand

A relationship occasionally
Will better a man and a woman
It should be no anomaly
If they've grown when it's done

When I stand reliantly
In love on some future day
Thoughts will remind me silently
Marissa showed the way

With that thought I'm atingled— my love

When the disparaging of my foes
And the altogether unsweet amount
Of my burdens pile high into unavoidable woes
I very often take account

And do consider my vices
That I mostly disdain
To maybe whiskey away my crises
Or shall I abstain?

What won't inebriate to soothe?
I consider what is mine to partake of
Violet soft and angel smooth
With that thought I'm atingled—my love

And if I'm fortunate enough you are near
As today in your bed so asleep
Watching you lie there my dear
Something inflames me to weep

Pretty curls flatter you there
As I gaze on your keepsake diamond ring
And I'm thinking how much I do care
For the girl that has made me a king

Troubles of the world float away
In this instant I'm looking at you
Your tenderness makes me feel gay
And needless to say I'm not blue

A thought in my mind really grips
While the sunlight streams in from above
Why not gallantly steal a kiss?
With that thought I'm atingled—my love

Alone up here aloft of living's pall
Gathering remembrances of yesterdays made into now
I long to scatter them down there, beyond the river where
The dead dry elms touch out

Commingled with this wintry air, my thoughts like ashes fall
Oer visages of long ago which loom about

Of faces from the past and
Tragedies seen
Its, hard to oft continue,
The same I mean, life's painful scheme

Such recollections sometimes sail grey rivers while they wind
Through dark and shadowy regions down the canyons of my mind
Often leaving blight behind; Ah the memories so unkind
See those elms decaying down there. Everywhere.

Fields of Afternoon

To you whose spirit's dying
I dedicate this poem
If you' feel your spirit crying
And are utterly alone

If their malice is commanding
And they've slandered and accused
If no soul seems understanding
And your heart has—been abused

If the world seems a hornet
Meant to sting but never care
With the people who are in it
Let me tell you; I've been there

I have wandered as you wander
Freighted heavily with rue
With a psyche wrought with squalor
In it's emptiness; like you

There's a certain shade of twilight
That oppresses like a tomb
At the pinnacle of midnight
The epitome of gloom

When you've lost somebody cherished
Whom your heart will not discard
There's a part of you that's perished
And your souls forever charred.

I remember so the fields
Of my home, when still a boy
In the dusk my memory yields
To that time when life was joy

That they've passed seems quite unreal
For their voices ring so loud
And the love that I still feel
Will be never disavowed

But my one love is a cover
To protect me from the cold
I will never love another
Should she pass before I'm old

When the world is a nightmare
In it's bitterness and hate
I can always find a friend there
Through the solace of my mate

Though her love has deeply, gladdened
I have looked into her eyes
And mysteriously been saddened
Even love like our love flies

During the crispness of the, autumn
In' the cold and echoed air
How I hold her to my bosom
She. is, precious.; she is rare:

And I'll hold her even stronger
In that cold and distant day
When acquaintances no longer
Fill our lives and pass away

While we walk the night together
(Through the fields of afternoon)
How I cherish and adore her
Grandness. passes all too soon.

Tired Man

He's worked hard all his life
But nobody thanks him
His wife passed away last fall
He honors and sings her a hymn
At her grave site once In a while

The friends that he knew have died
The friends that he loved so well
The young in his locality
Say He's as useless as hell
And his old morality

A widow across the way
Swears that his mind has gone
For speaking so much of his wife
And failing to start a new bond
A new wife; a new life

Bitterness seems the bounty
For the good life he has led
More loneliness ever he's known
Morality seems to be dead
(He's left alone)

But his hurt and tired spirit
Have' molded and shaped his way
With memories he has kept so fond
He holds them this very day
(And senses the great beyond)

The Majesty Of Silence

Thoughts with poignant care
Or lyrical abandon
Flair and flourish there
And come at random
In the silence

I have felt more like a king
My reasoning
A heightened thing
It's seasoning
The silence

Silence is a sedative
To calm the jangled nerves
A wonderful reprieve
And peace of mind it serves
The silence

Shadowed birds ascend
Beyond the fields at dawn
And hopeful fancies fend
Away the hurt and wrong
In the silence

When I recreate
Dreams the mind can make
And alleviate
Weariness and ache
There is silence

Yes, I have felt
More like a king
My majesty
A quiet thing
It comforts me
(The silence)

August Traveller

The night you loved me,1 captured the stars
The constellation Hercules
I drank of the milky way
And drew the shaft of Pericles

To bound a jet stream for Venusian piers
And trek a purple mist
That split the rift of light years

Alpha Centuari, Orion, and a sea of worlds beyond
Spots of neon!

I clasped a comet and followed it down
To skirt Diana's gown
Vacuumed regions of soundless sound

I leaped from the comet and out of the dark
My new steed the west wind; My song was the lark
My passions were pierced by the ocean's foam
I rode the west wind home.

Empathy With A Warm Woman

To touch the pith of a woman's soul
Someone warm and receptive and keen
With rapport and with wit in the night
Oh what a sensuous delight!
It's the time that I feel whole
(The happiest moments I've seen)

To reach a woman who reaches out
With her mind and her heart and her arms
Who with empathy touches me too
It's the time that I feel all new
What living is all about
The depth of two spirits; their charms

To kiss her mind and her warm warm lips
To be loved by her mind and her heart
It's a time when the bodies intense
And the physical passion immense
The gloom of the soul is eclipsed
And a terrible word is apart

Morning Distance Runner

Following a graceful gait like light
Passing as a shadow oer somber summer fields
Summer meadows, Summer meadows, through the meadows

Leaves adrift and flaccid, falling fallen
Billowy breezes blowing softly blowing
Easy breeze and easy footsteps flowing
Onward, Onward through the morning coming

Skylark hears the crunching passing oer
Now ascends beyond the morning clover
Oer a bridge whose waters show a sheen!
Whooshing oer planks and now those footsteps comming keen

Jogging oer gravel paths sodden
Fisherman was winking, nodded
Dusty dirty road getting in your eye
Overhead a pale yellow morning sunlit sky

Stream is flowing faster, currents icy, waters silver
Flowing farther following forth
Beyond the reaching river

Asphalt surface solid, quickening stride
As in a trance a surface seeming many miles wide
Warming currents of the sun; noon day tide

Currents oer meadow. Ascending hillside on
A gait like light, a shadow down the valley far beyond

The Conqueror

His blood burns with the intensity
Of a dancing bull in ancient Crete
He is courageous to the immensity
Of his all consuming feat

Where the conqueror roams
On distant lands uncharted
One hears the grievous shrieks and moans
Of battles started

Strewn with glorious corpse after glorious corpse
Is the battlefield wake of he
Who gallantly heroically warps
The pages of history

Have you known him in a school lesson
Cutting throats in guise of glory?
Leaving foes without concession
Or didn't it tell that story?

High and mightily he embarks
Brutally to beset
Blood and gore are grisly marks
Of his every conquest

The formula of a regimental!
War machine is fear
Battle is not sentimental
Victory brings no tear

And sad it is the past's not more
Than its lustful marrow
Of countries greedily fought for
With saber gun and arrow

So proud bastions pray be strong
Be prepared to die
History somehow seems all wrong
And I'm asking why

Innocence in youth I've felt is grand
Cotton candy commingled with sunlight
Starlight sprinkled faintly on the sand
Of a mystical shore on a restful night

Radiant dreams and windswept plans
Blown by awakening time
Evolving as the boy into a man
And the girl into something sublime

Holding hands on a lapping lake
Two will revel the warmth of youth
He'll be taciturn for her sake
In discovering quiet truth

Life is growing through things we share
Vicariously as we go
The verdant young learning to care
Obtaining maturity's glow

Like an oak towering up in the sun
Seeking stature through sunlight in the meads
Youth will flourish becoming as one
With a friend or a lover which it needs

Through their critical epoch the young
Need acknowledgment in the eyes
Of another and rapture among
Ethereal beckoning sighs

Thence to blossom as flowers in the spring
With their love as a calyx unfurled
Attaining adulthood to bring
Radiance to the world.

Beginning A Letter

It's the devil's instigation
At least it seems to be
This sorry situation
That's taken you from me!

No sooner were we beginning
A close affinity
Than destiny took you winging
You've travelled across the sea

There are many doubts in me now
Will you remember what's been?
IS it just me who cares and how
Long before I see you again?

It nags me because of my pride
Perhaps I meant nothing to you
But I think of you still at my side
What should I do? I

The nights are so long. How I reminisce
Of wanting to kiss you but came
Merely so close but imagine that kiss
Deep in the night just the same

So how do I start this letter?
Will I give myself away?
A fool knows no better
Than saying too much. They say

Foolish men do the dealing
The cool ones won't rush in
And usually show no feeling
Yet, somehow always win

But I'll just do my best with this pen
And probably play the fool
For I'm wondering so how you've been
Dear you, ...

When I Look At Her

When I look at her
I see attractiveness
I hear the wind blow
In the trees
The swirl of leaves
And I know
That I love her

But when I look at her
In her eyes
She is vulnerable
So much a child
(Intelligent child)
It Is so
That she needs me

And when our eyes meet
It seems endless
Two hearts suspended
In a glance
The look is love
We are one
As Intended

And the Rains Come Softly

All lives have their nuances
The little things that fall
With bad or good influences
Upon us all

They come so soft at times
We hardly know
But while the number climbs
They take their toll

We realize their aftermath
But can't avoid their fate
They swiftly while within our path
Accumulate

The elemental rains that rinse
We cannot them avert
But nuances we can't evince
Destroy our hurt

Were man to hold his fate supreme
And be denied his cloud
Of grim misfortune then I deem
His ego would be bowed

It's easier to take one's lot
When reasons can be given
Mentioning the luck we've got
Comes from ill winds driven

The rains today have purified
For I was not inclined
Anyway to toil outside
And I rest resigned

On Humor

Humor I think in its finest sense
Is a flippant remark at another's mistake
Cutting down quick the needless suspense
While causing a heart not to ache

Humor should be in a person's behalf
Not thoughtless or sneering or vile
With amity behind that laugh
Or uplifting smile

Now, I'll say not it can't be absurd
Or wild or rapidly paced
As long as the one who has heard
Has his ruefulness erased

I believe that our jovial, flair
Needs tact and warm cordiality
So it's obvious that we care
For all in our vicinity

Humor is quite a delicate art
But many men are not delicate
They defile it with their heart
Or violate it with smut

For good humor's linked with class
Or knowing to laugh or not to
Who ever a man is; he's crass
If humor's his sword of ridicule

I love a man who laughs at his errors
But never humiliates others
He's the salt of the earth and a person who cares
And all men are his brothers

But there's just one more point I should add
Humor can be a disaster
If the humor's misleading, it's bad
Lo! An elephant once called me sir

He asked, is the grand canyon deep?
I replied, No it's nothing, just peanuts
Now, I shudder to think of his leap
(This will always be on my conscience!)

Those who follow sport or
The various other dramas of human existence
Are often very poor
At determining excellence.

And I know, for my old friend Deke
Was a performer out of the greatest mold
But what they did to him makes me weak
And my blood run cold.

He became a prizefighter
Not of choice but of necessity.
And in youth he was lighter
With much grace, you see.

But the truculence of his years
Brought weariness to him such
That I was confirmed in my fears.
He had lost his touch

Now, I'm not a fan of prizefights;
On them I'd urge a permanent ban.
Yet, for Deke I'd not censure their heights.
He was just a mighty decent man.

He had wizardry and style in that ring,
Fighting just enough to make
A decision for himself that was a thing
Of beauty when he lost it was a handshake.

He tried not once to hurt or ride a foe.
I delighted in his style and his class.
How it hurt him when he saw the crimson flow.
There was not a thing about him that was crass

And even as a seasoned pro, his style
With authoritative seconds who were brash
Was to take advice with humbleness and smile.
And with people who were rude, He'd never clash

This is how I see him, now: As an old pro
Who was humble, keen, and not at all pugnacious
For a pugilist who'd taken many a blow.
This man was gracious.

The speed of the man had made him once, most feared.
He'd win on points not hurting an opponent.
So, the champs in his division readily steered
Away. They made him hunt.

They ducked him till he lost most of that speed
And he also lost so many fights it hurt.
I quit coming to his fights to watch him bleed.
He was getting more inert.

Only then he got his venture at the title
As a trial horse against the brash young champ
Who was swift and strong and arrogant and vital
And taunted Deke through seven weeks of camp.

The crowd was loud but I made nary a sound
The night they fought.
And it was in the second round
Deke got caught.

The champ battered Deke against the ropes
Calling him a bum and having fun,
Until the round's last seconds when Dekes hopes
Were smashed into oblivion.

But while the crowd erupted in a roar
I knew the only worthy, true performer
Was the crumpled beaten lump upon the floor.
And Deke would fight no more

Of Life and Of Love

Life, What do I know of you?
Your contradictory nature
Shouting at us
With benevolent expectations flirting so
Seductively while you lead us astray in the
Bloody Bloody wars. The tragedies all in all
How do they add up?

Though you have your aspects which can't
I don't feel, be forgotten. The
Sweetness of the kiss, the first kiss and the robin of spring
You devil, you are sweet and deceitful
Both. Perhaps it is your dark side helping us appreciate
The light.

And oh, people;, how they slander and
Bereave us for how many wield their hearts
Earnestly for righteousness and truth. They the people
Of a two fold countenance
Inducing ere deceiving, Oh,
But love doth have a way and it is love
Which causes all the tidal waves of squalor and despair
To subside beneath its' curiously
Bland and ancient song
For it, I suppose, is the bad
That makes the good worthwhile

I'll Run Like the wind through the country

I'll run like the wind through the country
Tonight when the sun is set low
And I'll run while the wind is about me
Though It shrilly engages me so

I will think quiet thoughts that are peaceful
While 1 glide in the gloaming, near night
And my spirit will surely be zestful
Like a seagull's itinerant flight

I will ponder my homeland about me
That was fashioned by him, from above
(Just how easy it is to adore thee)
And these acres and acres of love

I'll consider the mother who bore me
And my kinfolk dispersing, even now
Who are going away yet I feel we
Must meet again; this I vow

While I run like the wind through the country
I'll think of the woman that's mine
(How much and how deeply I love thee)
(Thy vestal sweet kisses of wine)

When running like wind in the evening
My matins will come ere the morn
With thoughts of thanksgiving I'm bringing
(My spirit will ne'er be forlorn)

A Multitude Of Form

A daisy defying the rain
It's beauty abounds through the storm
A strong man considered insane
He dares to be tender and warm

Motherhood valiant protecting
Going that extra mile
Tired and worn and erecting
Character with a smile

Starving and destined to die
A fugitive hopeless in flight
Refuses to maim on the sly
A week man with food in the night

There once was a man so forgotten
By others he knew not his name
Humbly he shares his begotten
Glory and runaway fame

A person they slander and shove
In misunderstanding and hate
Confronts them with kindness and love
Wisdom compels him to wait

Blind, she has helped them to see
With visions she has deep inside
The pessimist had to agree
Walking away—(He cried)

A traveler taught there is danger
In helping the wayward forlorn
Pacifies many a stranger
A multitude of form

The sunlight Eros

Through the forests of my passions comes
The sunlight Eros
Spawning incredible sums
So near to my heart, so close
Whose wings have shown me worlds new
So clear to my spirit, dear
Upon my honor I eschew
All unimpassioned thoughts I peer
Into the future far and near
(Eternity) And without fear
This uttered in solemnity
Through Eros I will fly there

The House

An ordinary house to some
But I pass it
With a tear forming in my eyes
Every time I come
Near it

There are other folks living there now
Driving by I
Consider they must think me odd
That I drive so slow
And even stare

They were wonderful old people
With love for each other and
The entire world; It
Was absorbed by me
In that house

I see it still
With my memory all sweet
The veranda; the kitchen
But mainly that livingroom
Of their love

I remember every nook
And every room within that house
How they saw me and themselves
In a kind and tender way
I loved them so

I am incredulous, yes
That they stand no more
Hand in hand by their garden
Or moving in the yard
Glowing

Those children make me sad
For regression isn't fun
I have walked where now they walk
And the world's turning cold
Without them

The Bars of Late Evening

When I travel the bars of late evening
It is not that I'm wicked or vile.
I am foolish perhaps but I'm seeking
A woman with depth in her smile

A woman with eyes that are lonely
Who is quiet and passionate too.
She's wise and will understand me,
So I'll feel uplifted and new.

This woman whose presence I'm needing
Hasn't pretense and doesn't make airs.
She's deep and she's not misleading.
Her eyes will say warmly she cares.

Her spirit will be revealing,
With eloquent words rich and kind,
The good and the bad she is feeling,
Letting me into her mind.

And so, we will know one another
Because she'll allow it to be
My looking so far inside her
And her looking into me.

A deep and a warm understanding
Might come as a token of this,
Because she is not demanding,
So softly our lips may kiss.

And our meeting will ever be treasured,
While saying goodbye in a sigh.
The affinity will be measured
By the radiance in our eyes.

The regretfulness for a shower

The regretfulness for a shower
That I have is the discourse
Of my mind that speaks intensely most of an hour
With influence from the water and its force

All this water coming hard
Seems to catapult my mind
To a past 1 can't discard
And it brings out many images left behind

while the steam is greatly warming me with its heat
I focus on the pain in romance I've had
Yet, I feel that life is bittersweet
Wondrous Joyous, sorrowful and sad

And it will stay diverse I'm sure
Like the water swift and stern
That seems restless and. demure
Life's a patterned driven circumstance meant to turn

This torrid shower is trembling me
With aspirations for my date this eve
But I'm troubled in my memory
Of a woman who did deceive

Like a wash of pure cold water tingling down
She left me cold
Though as this mist around
A void assails a man whose never bold

Will she tenderly my dream
Hold me close and start a tie?
Challenging shower do you deem
That she won't or never will unless I try?

Stone in a pond

A stone dropped in a pond
Makes ripples go beyond
They undulate with force
Of course

A baby after birth
Is forced to find its worth
To seek its farthest shores
Opening doors

The place the stone has hit
Is vivid quite a bit
But farther from that spot
It's not

The babe is much revered
But as his life is reared
The man is often ignored
Not adored

Away from impact's place
The ripples slow their pace
The current undulated
Gets complicated

The man no more a boy
Sees life as more than joy
While broader are frontiers
With the years

The Winged Horse

When the dull ceaseless things of existence
Tide into my day 'till I'm totally bored
I have but one viable resistance
That is to try to unleash
Some of the things my imagination has stored

I can imagine a beautiful maiden
A sprightly maiden with incredible powers of humor and charm
Beckoning with persuasion
To a place beyond the stars
Where she falls into my arms

This imagination is a winged horse, a protuberance
In my head that begs exit—occasionally
But often I cannot do this at once
With the toil or monotonies of the day
Until finally . . . .

There comes an occasional hour
When stress has been strangely subsided
My mood is not dour therein lies a power
Of mind that is flexibly rare
When on paper I have confided

Insensitive dull unimaginative entities appear no more
There are only the wistful and the warm
As my heart emanations while I sore
To mysterious realms not so shadowy
Because of their form

Walking Home

This makes me feel like I'm a boy again
Walking to my neighborhood because my car
Broke down while leaving work confound it though
And these roads are as dusty as far

This night air's a kind of a memory
Hard on my senses and the dark
Falls like the dust from the road on me
I seem so detached from my cares

It really makes me wonder, by golly
Why I overlook—these things
Each house and street have a personality
And a world of thought it all brings

I can almost imagine being a kid, again
And look at those kids over there
This sidewalk is like a bridge to the past
Ah, this night air!

I'd better get going though, it's late
She'll be wondering, yes, waiting, of course
This is enjoyable in its way but I hate
Having to walk so darned far!

There's the highway ahead, finally
But I still have so far, after that
Lord, walking at night is lonely
I wish I were home

These fields are so confounded somber
I wish I could fight this mood I'm falling into
Those-houses back there were friendlier
(Honey I'm coming, I love you)

That other neighborhood, house for house
Makes me think of when I was younger
The personality of my house and her house, too
(Dear God, I'm so glad I found her!)

My lord! It's finally conceivable
There's the old neighborhood not too far ahead
I wonder what she's doing; if she's still up
I don't doubt she's in bed

I don't think I could love again
God, I hope I never get the chance
She's as singular to my heart as my parents have been
One mother; one father; one her

A Place

In my innermost mind like a melody
lie the vestiges of a place
And they hang like eternal perfume, their ecstasy
Is the harmony of love's grace

Upon the redeeming
Pathways of incessant time
Will my psyche' s once foreseeing
Make real this clime

Beyond the sorrowful logic of all earthly thought
To recessions in my mind where lies beauty
Indignation dies out through this vestibule sought
In deeper dreams of tranquility

Here passes my thoughts to a spiritual region
Of love for the ones of this land
Exhibit a candor though with an adhesion
To kindness that's modestly bland

And an affable meaningful utterance
Of wisdom expounds from each face
They glow with their grandness I shudder once
At the thought of forsaking this place

A bright divination is here
Built upon trust love and praise
A habitat splendid and pure
Past the vagueness of cynical haze

This seems far away though conceiving
One might probe its mysteries
Through pain if one lives it, believing
One might find its certainties

Vacation

Extraneous work becomes
But; building your elation
It's here relieving doldrums
That long sought vacation

A trip to the shore in a fifty-five ford
And awaited moments out among
The spraying breakers so adored
When you and her were young

Appear you've set your sights
On cold trout streams or tennis courts
Gay summer nights
Or mountain resorts

With no concern but scurrying
Thither to do it all
Relatives will be worrying
Wondering what you saw

But for now you concentrate
Fully aware in knowing
Preparation can't wait
You've got to get going

Camping equipment and tennis shoes
Are packed for a long long ride
Yes, you can feel the blues
Of the work a day world subside

And no, your not concerned or
Anxious of fees you'll pay
This is something you've yearned for
Through many a month and day

Ah, your woman's impatiently beckoning
You give a last hurrying sigh
Till your hand on the wheel is steadying
Vibrant winds blow by

Bad woman passing of a long ago time

She was a kept woman and they frowned on her
Because her life was pock marked in sin and yet I
Remember her as a young lady, deformed, telling me that
She would know just one true love in her life and
Cherish him forever and ever and never
Love again though the lord might wisp him away long afore
Her time like the white swan clouds above us in the wind. Still she would never
Love again. And I was a young lad and did not understand

Clouds, dark clouds followed her in shadow all the days of her life and
Her deformity only grew worse and her ugliness brought no suitors;
Nor did her wit for she was never gifted, or pretty,
Nor wealthy or very wise though as a boy I thought her wiser
Than the young men who forever passed her by, scaring her with scorn
And I cried on her shoulder.

Her mother willed she attend the university with each and every other belle
Passing each year arm In arm with some handsome escort before them on the sidewalks
To the university until one day she felt beyond them all in years though—
None the less, they rejected her anyway and she ventured in to her thirties
Scraping away at small jobs barely enough to support her mother, often not;
When one day in her mid thirties I saw her go away with an old man many many years her senior to care and watch over him, she told me,
In another town
And I was a young man and did not understand

And the years flowed away like the raindrops of the sidewalks we had walked
In the rain; When once whispering she told me of regretting all those women,
Those who tore their husband's memory away;
For they married many times
And alas, I found a lover much more lovely than I'd dreamed
In my fondest dreams; And oh, her eyes were blue,
Azure blue as were my son's. And he favored me; He did
And I passed into my forties unafraid
But bad rumors fell as sin upon my son
And he asked me one day truly dad was she
Bad the one they found upon the grave of her—"
Mother in that town not far away
Did she die a death deserved and of the coldness of the night?

And my heart grew greatly saddened while I turned away a tear
Trickled slowly as I told him; She had perished not of that,
Not of cold but she had known a broken heart
"And she's passed away like white swan clouds. I hope she's found her love"
But he was young and could not understand

If I Were Caught In Time

I can sometimes imagine going
Back through time and being caught there
On a night when the wind is blowing
A time warp is my lair
And it is dark

Although I'd feel it's mystery
While wandering intrigued
The dust of a long lost city
Would leave me quite besieged
With pangs

If I were alone in the past
And fettered away by time
I'd be lonelier much than a wind chilled moor
My emptiness sublime
If I were caught in time

All the perspective I've had
That's good seems to come from her
The past would be horribly horribly sad
If I were caught forever
In a time before my time

Some ancient street would call
There'd be murmuring. There'd be laughter
Unheard; how my heart would fall
Knowing I'd never see her
(Again)

My son

His eyes are the color
Of fresh blue skies at early day break
They light up my life with his laughter
That sparkles from his throat like church bells
On an eager bright day.

His face has the making
Of summer meadows, apple sauce, and innocence
And a long lost awakening
That I can only feel
And have again, in him.

There is not a trace of animosity.
Pettiness, pride, or meanness in him.
He gives to the world sincerity
And a simple delight that's touching,
And I want to hug him,

I don't want to believe it
That he'll ever be hurt by life.
No, there's not even a bit
Of hurt in him now, and I'm sure
He will never hurt.

I know it by those wonderful eyes
That have a crafty appeal for one so young.
And I have never seen that little guy disguise
His feelings when they're good.
His heart is sweet.

And if I have my way,
By all that is tender and holy in this world
He will surely have his day
And retain much of that splendor
God knows, I love him.

Ebon Steel— from a time long ago

Ebon came and went
Like the shifting winds
I knew not what was meant
He said he'd sinned

Ebon had no heart they said
Ebon had no feel
Ebon was as good as dead
Mr. ebon steel

And yet he spoke so softly
Whenever he talked to me
His manner was never lofty
Like other folk; I could see

And I could never understand
Why people called him dim
Ebon was strong of heart and hand
Yet, they laughed at him

And Mr. Steel was kind
We passed the hours
People said he had no mind
Still Ebon built me towers

Far of castles in the sky
Dreams; Yet their romance
Carried me with a knowing eye
As melodies do enhance

The heart within a young one's soul
His spirit made me strong
(people brought him thoughtless woe)
Their cruelty was wrong

One day he disappeared
Leaving me alone
Gone forever, I feared
While my heart, a stone

Sensed he was running somewhere far
Where life would never follow
Maybe to a different star
What had made him hollow?

And after Ebon had gone
No one would tell me why or where
While I spent many an idle dawn
Hurting but they didn't care

Faith was in my favor through and many times I asked
About him believing in my friend
Keeping my feelings masked
(thinking they'd tell the truth about him then)

For emptiness is a condor flying
Through disconsolate nowhere realms
Where blossoms bloomed are dying
And vast, desolate, dreary elms

It was like I'd known already
When I finally heard
From a man whose laugh was steady
Cruel and absurd

Ebon nearly killed someone
Who'd ridiculed his mother
While saying that she was like her son
And would not bear another

Where Ebon's gone I'll never know
But, perhaps some day
We'll chat amidst the heaven's glow
(There, no skies are grey)

There Is A Oneness

Meadows of sweet clover
Blown subtly with the wind
Or the solemn thought
Of sea and shore
Your kind and tender presence
Does convey
Are similitude's
Of our essence
When were one
In a fairy tale
So it seems
Any season
When your kiss
Makes us one

Death is a sweet gentle maiden

I have dreamt of the ocean's foam
Enshrouding a woman in mist
Through this windy region to home
I am led for I can't resist.

Death is a sweet gentle maiden
Who doth love all men the same
And walks with them to Eden
Whispering their, name.

Her presence is narcotic
She induces away the pain
The love of her heart is a tonic
This sweet and gentle swain.

Amidst the starry twinkling
Of her eyes that are soft and fond
No spirit can have an inkling
That indeed it has passed beyond.

And one day I'll surrender
For she thinks to really care
She's soothing and she's tender
Compassion is her lair.

With liniment and lullaby
And arnica and song
She'll soothe me in that sunny sky
Where right is made from wrong.

She'll venerate my presence there
I'll kiss her lips of course
She'll quell my soul with words so rare
And steal away remorse.

In living there's a loneliness
That's eating at my mind
It's misery and emptiness
I'll one day leave behind.

She'll lead me to eternal love
Where angels sing my name
They'll calm me in that land above
Ecstatic that I came.

She'll say the sweetest things to me
And I'll return them too
With lofty words of ecstasy
She'll kiss away my rue.

With mild mercy in her face
Her love will push through time
Transcending all of time and space
So utterly benign.

A realm where love's an edict
And shared supreme by all
Will welcome spirits once lethargic.
Who heed her maiden call.

Your smile

In the morning when an ocean
Of sunlight cascades me
My every little motion
Seems vain against my lethargy
While I move against the covers
To rise and face the dawn
I remember we are lovers
While you're moving like a swan
And with your smile

And how truly overwhelming
The morning light would be
Were you not amid my waking
Or sweet in memory
If I woke to know you parted
And took away your warm
I'd be hurt before I started
In the dreary mask of morn
Without your smile

But this morning it's my notion
As sunlight surrounds me
Your laughter is like a potion
Cascading down the hallway
And those footsteps coming nearer
Portending of your love
Make it altogether clearer
I will never tire of
Your smile

Waif

Little man with heart of stone
Why doth thou wander all alone
Without a home?

No dowager arms to take you in
To still the aching hurt within?
Ah worldly sin!

Encircling winds about you shrill
Assail you with a dreadful chill
You're gravely ill!

And hath no mother's loving eyes
Allayed you from these stormy skies?
The world's demise!

Has respite not the least assuaged
Though terrible icy winds have raged?
No soul has paged!

An old man though could not create
Just sustenance or mitigate
Your cruel fate

For ancient feeble bones can't care
For what the world's done out there
It's own despair!

Encircling though are thoughts afar
Of amities life shant ever mar
Like a comforting star

Brisk memory winds within construe
Of a child adrift and full of rue
Just like you

And thank the lord his hearts' not died
Your legacy won't be denied
Do come inside!

When My Love Was Young

Were not the green fields greener still
When my love was young?
Did she curtail the autumn's chill
In their hearts that hung
Near the window sill?

The flowers and the skies of blue
Saw the young girl grow
Playing in the morning dew
With a smile aglow
And how my lady grew

Overcast days were visioned bright
When my love was young
By sheltering ones whose loving sight
Watched her out among
The peonies in the night

The lingering rains were rhymes of cheer
When my love was young
To her parents and friends who held her dear
Love was softly sung
When my girl was near

And presently hence my heart's been stung
From its sting 1 have given a vow
All my love and my passions I've flung
For 1 am even happier now
Than when my love was young

Yes, This Is What I Want

A woman in the night I want to meet
Someone who will share her mind and then
Dig inside of mine with words; oh sweet!
And understand my mind more than a friend

This woman in the night I want to know
Tenderly and sweetly in a stream
A passion stream with empathetic glow
That takes us like two lovers in a dream

This woman, very deep, might know my mind?
Dearly while disclosing much her own
Then imagination might unwind
And fly us off with inhibitions blown

A woman who is common yet profound
Earthy who will get inside my thought
Clinging to me lifting me from ground
And I will cling to her with love I've caught

A woman with imagination too
Wild but reliable and sound
Fantasizing things to ease our rue
We'll wield words which lift us—heaven bound

It hath made, better the years

There is some good in
The hearts of all men
Christmas makes open
This truth so that 'when
Those who hold hope and a steadfast believing
Try to foresee that complete love is near
Christmas will help in their needed conceiving
That a pure world will appear

This special time of the year has given
A peace to my soul many times through decades
Happiness comes as each snowflake driven
For, beyond Christmas, it fades

My heart remembers the joy of boyhood
Comforting thoughts of my folks' security
Though I've reproved them at times how I would
Certainly say they have loved me

Pondering back through my life accessing
Christmas, I know, hath made better the years
And in recalling the love of those passing
Christmas renews my tears

An Old face

Memory is like a thing unpleasant and divine
That touches upon the corners of the mind
An unexpected warm yet subtle sting
That whispers oh so lightly on the heart strings
(But reaches of so deep)

His voice was like a subterranean echo
As it "touched upon the wind and said hello
Unexpectedly 1 turned as might a swimmer
Who is startled by a voice above and near
I was startled by the past

The unpretentious warmth so warmed my spirit
And the matter of fact yet casual way he said it
Was refreshing to my mind and blew away
The heaviness and strain I felt that day
(I felt that day)

Young Widow

Young and so alone—So alone
She finds the world's focus quickly spinning
As one who'se been so hurt before she's grown
All seems ended—at the beginning

His memory has whispered to her often
Though intangible as sirens in the wind
His person is forever in a coffin
And rue and deep depression must rescind

Yet the amatory fragrance of the lilacs
Reminds her of the first bouquet he gave
Her reverence is with her as she walks
And places these with care beside his grave

Like a flower blooming early in the winter
Left bereaved to face compeers again in spring
She's a woman-now, but he's no longer with her
Maturity's a melancholy thing

Should I Live Forever

There is a kind of foregone conclusion
I must certainly resign myself to
That I will die and pass away is no illusion
All people do

I may go perhaps some sultry day in August
Or a cold and windy cloudy day in fall
Resignedly I face, this for we all must
Death betides us all

Yet at moments in my lifetime I endeavor
Having kissed my love or seen a flower in bloom
To immortalize myself and live forever
And betray somehow this malady of doom

Isn't living all important in its sweetness
And it's pleasures consummate beneath god's sun?
Isn't death a dreary demon in its fleetness?
Everyone has thought this and I'm one

There's a bounty to be taken out of living
In our formative years and aged years of wine
And a host of lovely memories from giving
To light up another's eyes and see them shine

Yet, the shade of the mimosa isn't given
At the polar cap so lonely barren and stilled
And our love and friends in late late years are driven
From this world till our stricken hearts are chilled

For with beauty life still bears its pain and fury
That we might accept death's coming peaceful call
Wise and contemplative as were weary
Knowing we have lived and done it all

Yes, my marvelous creator will recall me
As he wants the new to come and comprehend
So as many people know life as there can be
And he hopes I understand this in the end.

For the planet that we live on is not boundless
And to make room for another, this one knows;
God must bring us back to dust from which he found us
But he keeps us in the saving of our souls

There's A difference

Being troubled and insane, I say are two different things
The callous have stood like a rock of indifference
While the troubled rage and wrangle at the stings
Caused by the indifferent who are blind
Or throw stones

Being troubled and insane: I say, are not at all alike
The callous have stood like a mountain of callousness
While the hurt and stricken suffer sin or strike
Back at the indifferent who don't realize
Just what fools they are

Being troubled and insane, I say are opposites, oh yes
The callous have stood like a mountain of self righteousness
While the fallen plead in earnest for forgiveness
But how can they ever rise in heart again
If they're scorned and not forgiven?

Being troubled and insane, I say, are like two different doors
The callous will not open theirs and let you in
You've confessed your sins and opened yours
They have sinned like you but stand aloof
And say they're better

Being troubled and insane, I say are miles and miles apart
The callous won't confess their sins or let you in
Though you've opened up and offered them your heart
You've confessed your sins; they haven't—still you give your heart
They won't accept it

Being troubled and insane, I say, can join into the same
(when those who should love you and understand turn their backs)
And you must accept entirely, the blame
If they won't lay down their pride and help you back
How sane are they?

The Awakenings: Like Spring

A kiss! the first, the tenderest in a sense
Of a life time because it is the first
The fresh different stirrings; their young hearts immense
In a very real way, new birth

The rolling live meadows of green burning grass
See the young man with cheeks of ice cream
His first pair of spaudings; he runs after class
Through the fields of summer in a dream

But going back farther, remember
How he looked that invaluable day
The second, the minute, the hour
He lay by her side, that way

And her; in her tear-jerking tenderness
Beyond any words ever made
Holds him close to her ripening breast
While her husband's emotions cascade

Then fighting back tears, no longer
Wildly he sobs with his wife
An incredible moment to remember
With ardor, the rest of his life

Puberty, vague aches of manhood
A time when the heart does weigh
A trillion alternatives, yet, if I could
Only go back for a day

The emotions of youth are volcanic
Needing someone to understand
And the pulse rate is very quick
When merely he touches her hand

But all this is laughable later
When compared to the ultimate thing
Of a starry-eyed two at the alter
The thoughtful commitments they bring

The woman who once played jacks
The man who tagged triples and got dirty
The innocence of summer skies and back packs
Now a nobler maturity

There's a soul aching pang like a knife
Prickling spirit when I think of certain things
That are touchingly tender and once in a life
The awakenings, (ah the awakenings)—like spring

Another Spring

Do I detect a touch of thyme?
Thyme, thy fragrance gladdens.
I must still feel young for I'm
Caught by a certain madness

Rosebuds nod while winds touch gently
Somethings in the air.
All the more, these days, I sense thee,
Thou, my lady fair

An awareness of mind most piquant
Appends to me and prevails.
Of late I am delinquent
Of tasks, ah my diligence fails!

And pangs of love are paramount.
They supersede all thought
So glad I am true love I caught
Late grey years shall not daunt.

I see the forest sassafras
And long to touch its fruit.
While looking through this window sash
I vision pan and flute!

But turning, I can hear my love.
She's utmost wonder and
Her love warms like a woolen glove
Upon a chilly hand.

Another spring it is, but logic
In my heart seems sound:
Spring would forfeit much its magic,
Were she not around.

All Summer In Her Smile

Yesterday a woman at an ice cream shop
Startled me; the summer air was still
Her smile was like something from the long past
When summer never ended—if you will
Her manner was polite and she was matronly
But attractive and her eyes were warm as toast
They sparkled like the sunlight through a willow
And her smile was the thing remembered most

As a boy I often wandered in the summer fields
And I felt that every human was my friend
Like the clover of those meadows, long ago
Life was but a joy that didn't end
But I grew, alas, and found the smiles shadowed
There were many who were cynical and mean
And I confess I've grown that way myself somewhat
And my heart has somewhat faded, yes indeed

But somehow she renewed my summer joy again!
But a moment; but it shattered on my brain
Something in her unaffected smile
The intelligence and warmth so sweetly sane
Her inner glow was obvious, but more than that
She projected it to me; so much to say
She had noticed me and sweetly softly meant it
In the way she wished me well, that summer day

Scents

Jogging in the cool of the country air at night
The feeling is of freedom and a redolent delight
The vernal scent of balsam is immersing me, it seems
In a totalness of greenwood and the attitude of dreams

The winsome wind is sudden and laconic is its mood
With subsistence in a murmur and the country air exudes
With a fragrant scent of Jasmine while the night airs introduce
The myrtle and the Jonquil and the linden and the spruce

Restoration of my spirit is the midnight quietude
With its certain scents of flora and the verdure it imbues
Brindled shadows are abounding from the sylvan land around
The faint and lonely twinkling of the starlight hath no sound

Peculiar are the gravel and the dusty dirty roads
They seem to me like incense while their mysteries unfold
The rustle of a Poplar stirs my heartbeat while I run
Aromatic are the flora and the roads upon my lungs

The perfumes and the quiet of the hour that is late
Seem to pacify my spirit, I'm composed and so sedate
There's a sensuousness about it that intrigues and still I run
And I feel for the moment that with nature, I am one

Maiden Of The River Of Love

It is a sweet river
Quite like a lullaby it flows
Shimmering on forever
Windward and wistful it rolls
A lonely traveler
Is lonely no more if he follows
Where it goes

Good is a woman; a giver
If tender she is with her charms
River of love deliver
A lonely man into her arms
Here, he will find her
A maiden to shield him from harm
(Shield him from harm).

She is a sweet maiden
Kissing the loneliness from your lips
You who are sorrow laden
Feel her vaporous mists
You are the only one
Her vestal sweet features have kissed
Don't resist!

A Child And Nature

I'll not be quite as young again
As when I was a child
An alibi it is but then
My heart's a bit defiled

And though it's just a might, I'll say
It's very much apparent
To feign in knowing nature's way
Boorish I'd be and arrogant

What adult can comprehend
The magic of the dew
I'd be an actor to pretend
I knew what once I knew

The forest verdure oaks and pine
And rills so soft and still
Won't mystify me again nor the kine
That grazed upon the hill

A child has a knowing eye
Never too dull or proud
To overlook the radiant sky
Or the artistry of a cloud

When storm clouds brew and sprinkle rain
A child shows his poise
Through thunder he'll sustain
And revel in the noise

A rose is apparent bliss
I would be fallacious
To try to appear like this
A child is merely gracious

The time has passed when I
Can quite be one with nature
Although I sometimes try
And me in all my stature!

The Paradise Of Your Kiss

The quiet of your hush
Thrills me like the leaves
Of the aspen trees
Swelling in a rush
When you sigh with me

Darling I feel a yearning
In the silentness
While I watch discerning
Your wondrous radiance

And my heart is seared and burning
From your glowing countenance
While my lips are happily learning
Of the rapture of your kiss

Our reliance bears compliance
To a twofold tenderness
An ethereal gentleness

Hold me now in bliss and never
Fault the fever of our kiss
Or my fond and sweet caress . . .
And I'll love you dear forever
An endeavor born of this
Of the paradise of your kiss

The Velveteen Bat Slinger

In the outskirts of the solar system zeron,
On the lonely God-forsaken planet kaylite,
Came a broken spaceship like a fallen heron,
Much dissevered by inclement meteorites,
They that caused this craft of high design to veer on
Its premier flight of all appointed flights
And descend until its pilot felt much fear on
Kaylite, here, to spend his solar nights.

Why in heaven's name did fate betray him?
On this tyro mission fear was his already
And he landed in the night time, starry, dim,
When all that moved in traces of a levee
Were unappointed mists upon the rim
Of the planet's only moon or but a bevy
Of meteorites, he felt the chances slim
To see a human again. His heart was heavy

Far about the desolate place he scanned
A wearisome task, but he would not sit down.
Nervousness kept him moving so he planned
To scrutinize all he could until he found
If there was life upon this lonely land,
When all at once in terror he hit the ground.
A voluminous gale was shrieking and blowing sand,
Raising an eerie horrible sobbing sound!

The sandstorm like a God in wrath berated.
It wailed until he had to soliloquize,
Sobbing and saying he was surely fated
To die beneath these barren ungrateful skies,
Harder the winds came now and castigated
The spaceman until they blotted out his cries
And he felt, alas, incarcerated,
To perish here, yet, he opened wide his eyes.

Within some yards he saw a kaylite cave
And groped while he crawled like a madman to make it there.
Furrowing sand, he shrieked and began to rave,
Succumbing so close to the cave he could not bear.
He achieved it and had his spirit now to save.
The sandstorm had verified that there was air,
So he tore off his space suit, more the frantic than brave,
Revealing his cotton velvet underlayer.

The tall handsome man of velveteen was king!
But he realized he might ne'er see the earth again,
For how could he get his countrymen to bring
Liberation from this his probable end?
Of a sudden a phosphorescent bat took wing!
Like an arrow it shot by a shadowy darkened bend
And, after some others had circled above in a ring,
An idea cropped up in the velveteen man, right then!

The planetary gravity here was slight!
He could leap up and catch a bat or two if he'd try
And take them from out the cave to clasp them tight
And hurtle them as a beacon to the sky!
He hurtled them; he slung them with all his might!
He hurtled them with a cry so very high
And, while slinging the sparkling bats as a beacon light,
The indomitable spirit of mankind would not die.

Vivacious was his spirit in his youth
He roamed the wild countryside so free
He sought the flaming motives of his heart
And found his trade in keen vivacity!
And then he feel in love

He lived with her in passion many years
Conceiving from his love a son and daughter
And molded wife and family so nice
Her nourished all the three in love and laughter
And deep respect

And then came middle age, a second springtime
Approached him as his children moved away
He honoured this and held his wife the closer
Ennobling her still more with passing days
He loved her so

And as the years passed on he kept in touch
With his son and daughter the best he could
When he could not visit he would write them
When they needed he was there and understood
With word or deed

And just the same he was with friends or strangers
He did the best he could though sometimes wan
If even he was sick and not in spirits
He proved to be a thoughtful tender man
And showed much depth

But now the darkened latter years came on
The grey and cloudy years of introspection
His wife passed on to heaven, he was one
He stood alone with many deep reflections
And mourned his wife

His seventies brought on his final spring
Not only had his wife but all his friends
Gone on in death to meet, again, their maker
I wondered, is it here the spirit ends?
No, not with him

Instead of being bitter or unfriendly
He forged his heart with one more battle cry
And blessed his children's children though so lonely
He must have ached so badly but he tried
To give what he had

And now I often think that he decided
That we were more important than his rue
Oh grandpa I will always love you
(I will always love you)

This Stream Of Beauty

Now, I see her standing there
A tiara's in her hair
What a luminous gown of white
During this night

A far off stream with nebulous apparitions
Is summoning my volition
Shall not I stay in melancholy here?
I feel no fear

With the wind's vivacious lullaby breeze
Intermittent through these trees
Melodious is her step and fluently
To the woods I follow, secretly

My staid heart pounds; The bugs around me flit
This realm of foliage is very dimly lit
I hardly see
Phoebe in her orb is guiding me

The maiden there goes
Into the denser forest where it flows!
This panacea stream to cure my woes
(This loneliness that grows)

How chimerical this flora seems which blooms
Emitting its perfumes
Pervading me in mystery
And bland unusual piquancy

There's a palfrey sometimes taking me in dreams
To idyllic lands and starry glistening streams
But my waking thoughts expunge
My dream before I plunge

A precursor to my wakefulness is mire
That I lie in ere I wake; will this transpire?
An infinity is thought
This life has made me gravely overwrought

These rustling leaves!
They're trembling me my psyche now believes
That an amatory urging
Beckons and will be emerging

Murmuring conclusively to my trust
Shrill winds wail about me saying I must
Thrust into his forest old
Brave and bold

Senorita! Senorita! Where are you!
Salient one of love say not adieu!
Surreptitious lady come to view
(But there's nil but darkened hue)

Dolorous in the night I'm ruing
Deeper is this dark ensuing
Than I've ever felt before
O'er sylvan things my soul doth pour

There beyond the hemlocks
Where there's marvelous phlox!
Vapour rises, — (verily)
Laughter's floating merrily

Multifarious shapes and forms I cannot count
Dance about. This is the fount!
A codeine Dream? A sorcerer's scheme?
My radiant stream!

A spirit minx emerges
From the mist converges
Assuaging me in stride
We quietly glide

And tremulous is my heart were dancing
Gnomes and satyrs I'm not fancying
Guard this stream entrancingly
This stream of beauty

Simply Her

In this day of super sophisticated liberalism
Where old beliefs are torn and mocked by many
And our country seems a monument to negativism
It has often been a painful thing to see

The established things have faded in a concert
Of repugnant voices mean and immature
Its enormity and thoughtlessness has hurt
But I marvel at the simpleness of her

Her intelligence and worth is overwhelming
But she gives it oh so often like a child
When the world seems so hard and so misleading
I am lost amid a creature warm and mild

She loves me with a cunning and a humor
But so softly holds her hands within my hand
As if to make me feel I am stronger
I'm not, I know, but yes, I understand

She loves her country grandly with a sweetness
I would give my life to it because of her
She teases me but loves me with completeness
Like a child who is tender and secure

A Piquant Total Relationship

Spring in vibrant vividness has come on, once again
Like determined soldiers marching on and on
And its vigour and its earnestness says "do it if you can"
But my spirit's strength has tired and is wan

(My heart is far too desensitized by past involvements)
All the fruitless past relationships, I've known
Have dissolved through lack of empathy to sad annulments
Now I feel very very much alone

Oh, there is a sweeping sadness gone into my bones
Not just my heart, the limits of my reason
So far into my psyche like volcanic stones
Weighing a crushing weight into this season

But I can still sense spring's hopefulness
And the laughter of the young beneath its sky
But there's a burden to my heart that borders vastness
And a hurt that makes me shun to even try

But try I must for yet I feel the chance
That I'll find someone who's piquant to my psyche
Who is fresh and fun and witty to enhance
The deeper things inside that can uplift me

Yet, the shroud of past involvements are a myriad
Of shallow sensuality and pain
And I'm foolish, I suppose, with all the hurt I've had
To ever even think to try again

I have known too many women who can give themselves
Only with their bodies; they are shallow
Insensitive and lacking depth. My spirit delves
Into a thoughtful someone I can follow

But can I go this route, and say my heart's a virgin
And finally find someone who's simply right?
Is there anyone like this beneath the sun
Who will lighten up my soul amid this night?

Someone I'm attracted to so physically
But who also has a keen and thoughtful mind
Who perks me up in body; also spiritually
Together; and is sensitive and kind

Someone who can bathe my heart and make me bathe in hers
In a total way all fervid to the soul!
Who moves my body, heart, and spirits' pores
In a piquant total way that makes me a whole!

Run With Me— Love With Me— On This Day

Shall I love you in the morning
Or the middle of the night?
It is better without warning
With abandon hold me tight

Hold my hand among the miles
As we run along the lake
Making merriment with smiles
That illuminate our wake

With vivacity and wonder
Shall we shake the heavens down
With our hearts agog with thunder
As we run and hear them pound?

Though the air is crisp and icy
And the grey clouds pall the skies
Our sensations will be spicy
So much love within our eyes

And the storm's splenetic splendor
Will regale us the more
Serving merely to engender
Raptured hearts amid the pour

Gentle maiden. Mirthful maiden
Please then kiss the rain away
With my tears so heavy laden
That have bound me till this day

I Am A Simple Man

I am possibly guileful at various
Times and enjoy the raciness of an abandoned and possible
Wit as I laugh gleefully through the night in
Plausible abstract humor and
Whimsical and even complex thought patterns, perchance, but
The me I adore is a
Straightforward man in search of
The exacting thoughts of love of the one I love said
In that heart drumming sheer exhilarating manner
In the silence of the night with our two hearts blasting
With the heat of that simple emotion and displaying
It's profundity in the vast tenderness
Of our profound emotions

Wayward Girl

The blown sandy hair
That was tousled all fell'
To her shoulders on the roadside there
I bade her farewell

And her bright eyes were green
Like emerald skies
The wisest I've seen
Darting like fireflies

When she had told
Of her life that was free
And conversed while she rode
Down the highway with me

The season was fall
And I was twenty two
And had answered the call
Of wealth within my view

Though with all my ambition
Attaining me this
I sensed admonition
From this wayward miss

She warned me that life
Is a perilous thing
And a man needs a wife
To help him take wing

She had not loved before
But needed one lover
To love and adore
To cherish forever

And her ethics were good
She'd have stayed with me
I knew if she could
(Such affinity)

Alas, as it were
I could not bring
Myself to her
Hearing wedding bells ring

But now I am older and sadder too
And if I could go back—my heart would unfurl
Yes, I would love you, wayward girl

Out Near The Porch

I remember as a kid looking up from
The faucet at the back of the house near the porch
I felt as small as I could be
How totally did the night come
The stars were small explosions from a torch

How black was the night, an eternal molasses
And there seemed to be so very many starts in it
I felt as small as I could be
Yes, that's the way it was
A vast and boundless blackness, brightly lit

And oh, I looked up at that deep blackness
And at those pretty starry patterns
My little heart reverberated fast
The wonder of my soul was made immense
And it seems as if I noticed every star pattern

Yes, that little barefoot boy was surely me
And the universe was filled with awesome wonder
And I knew not who I was, then
I had no identity
And far too much to ponder

The faucet at the back of the house near the porch
I looked up at the night so icily still
My feet were bare and cold on the patio
But my heart was awed and scorched
(For it ached at the sight of a scene much beyond my will)

And the cars passing at night on the freeway
The magnitude and the vastness of those nights
I felt as small as I could be
Exactly exactly who was I
In the scheme of eternity?

The Man And The Girl

He was all man, virile poised and passionate
His friend was all woman but somewhere along the road
She forgot just what it was that made him love her
Emasculating him she withheld herself from him and shut
Off her support for what he was trying to do with his life, the weight
Was palling on his mind, he was confused and unsure

The girl was unsophisticated, plain, and straight forward
Without guile, great wit, and she was twenty three
But she knew just what it was that made him wanted
So desperately to love and feel adored
That night she loved him warm and unabashedly
All resistance left his heart and he was heated

Her kiss was warm and needful and it moved him
She pulled his body warmly to her body
Not a word was said, they kissed with tongue and fire
What happened to his mood that once was grim?
He felt secure, his bosom felt the beauty
And his passion was a hot electric wire

Midnight shed a shroud of pagan gloom
Phantom things in form of shadow filled my room
In the glaring candlelight
Irascible and lurid in the night

Piercing wails of the loon impaled the tide
Crackling breakers fell resoundingly and died
While in stealth a thing possessed
In writhing dread came creeping, 'Twas grotesque

Swirling leaves in moonlit whorls whence it crawled
'Twas my heart a palpitation pounding loud
And my candle knocked about
Sensational in toppling; it went out

Ventured I a shriek in terror; ere it screamed
Yowling horribly in blood lust and it seemed
To be driven by my dread
I lie languid so alone in my bed

Tumbling ever, evermore there, the room fell
Reeling farther, ever harder into hell
Cascading into shadow.

Thence my spirit danced a drowning pirouette
Plunging down in tides of trauma sweating wet
To my stairway now it crept
Having entered from the foliage, while I wept

Whence a clap of sounding thunder rumbled down
Rain drops danced in minuet upon the ground
Whining breezes made a sound
Of melancholy angels all around

And my pangs in propagation chilled me more
There I thought it cast in moonlight on the floor
Had I visioned it was there
In the cruel gripping fear of a nightmare

Jenny

Many summers since that day
Summers ago in June
All my thoughts have gone away
To a moment that ended soon

Of cypresses and green grass fields
And the radiant smile of
Jenny me memory often yields
To multiple thoughts of love

Pondering how her quietness
Brought spiritual warmth to me
How tenderness in itself could bless
And render my spirit free

For Jenny was nice as one could be
And as pure as a country brook
Mild and thoughtful often she
Could enamour me with a look

The rivulets of our young romance,
Impetuous with their force;
Carried us, yet, by certain chance
They never ran their course.

Like the colourful leaves that came to call
In our summer of restless youth
Infatuation could fall
To eventual pangs of truth

So I made a decision bittersweet
There were other loves I might know
Doesn't temporal romance help us meet
A love that's final?

In the moment my Jenny said goodbye
I felt the oppressive heft
Of the burden she bore and her asking my why
Saddened me when I left

Lo, my time of experience leaves me cold
And the tears in my eyes are still wet
Since Jenny, the years have showed
I haven't found true love yet

My Seventh Mirth

In accepting your heart;
I have held a rebirth
I have come into my own kind of happiness
I have found my special mirth

And all that I am
Or all I ever will be
I owe to you my love
For it was you who set me free

My spirit is an eagle
Free and proud and gushing
Lo, when I'm with you now
My very soul comes rushing

And my total self comes on
As a wave not faltered by the wind
Or as a waft of whitecaps
So gentle from within

And while away my heart is gay
For it is certain love
The dark skies linger never dear
My heart strings are a dove

No one so true and gentle
And loyal of love as you are
I feel quiet restfulness
And my heart was wondered far

Oh I know that you are you
And I'll say this for the record
My plateau has been reached
And it's all of your accord

And with the years and with the days
And with the months and hours
I'm happy, darling, happier
More grateful to be yours

The Sophisticated Man

They said he was a simple man
He didn't strike back when
They battered him with insults
Derided him and then
Spat on him

What kind of a fool
Is he the women all said
He has no art, I bet he's never
Had a woman in bed
He's a simpleton alright

But no! Let me say this
With all my fiercest pride
He was an individual
With substance inside
(He was a man)

No, he would never
Fight their fire with fire
And surrender his dignity
He had something higher
Than they understood

Like that night for instance
When the thugs were beating
And kicking me till I might have died
But his presence was defeating
For them

He strode with an abandon
At the thugs in that twilight
With his look that made them wince
They gave up without a fight
They ran

And he laughed at the thugs
(The stout-hearted fellow)
And cursed but was tender
Contrite and mellow
With me

And the stranger left
He left as he had came
A different sort of man—to them
But I will never bet he same
I want to be like him

Spring Fever

A cavalcade of women
Prancing upon my mind in a coruscated flash
Like the new and warmer sun
Rearing with audacity through my window sash
Corresponding my heart beat leaving me
Restless as a swallow leaving its nest
This is spring in all its glory
A season more compelling than the rest

When grand designs of grandeur
Leap disturbingly through my mind like currents
Reckless and unbridled with desire
My somber senses offer no deterrent
A restless raging cauldron is my heart
Coquettishly it asks, "oh, can you grow?"
Fermenting me it tries to pull apart
The cobwebs from my mind and grandly sew

The Old Man

I felt the weathered wisdom of his years
Death had not summoned him yet
This old man recounting, near to tears
His long life fading, as a sunset

The mellow appeal of his tones
Comforted me; he spake
In celestial ardor though his bones
Had wearied within time's wake

The gnarled body shuddered with the strain
Of long years in the hayfields
Remembering times that brought him pain
The barren years; Their pitiful yields

The wily sagacious spirit, yet
Kindled him I conceded
Through arduous labor not to fret
A Bible was all he'd needed

A portraiture hung above him high
Upon the veranda wall
His tired eyes asked: How could she die
So young statuesque and tall?

She was the only woman he had wed
He honored her and raised two sons
Respectable boys and good; he said
He loved those young ones

Alas, the war had killed his eldest son
And smallpox the other
But his love life, in honor of her, was done
He would not have another

The breezes blown into the porch
Quieted me; He spoke
Of his wonderful friends that like a torch
Had vanished and passed, as smoke

A long life had wrought much pain
Yet, his wholesomeness made him glow
Bitterness was against the grain
Of the thoughtful old soul

Yes, I'd sensed the weathered wisdom of his years
When death had not beckoned him yet
Now the old man's memory still endears
His long life's found its sunset.

To My Older Lover

The gulf of personalities
Melted off like dew
When separate realities
United—(and I loved you)

Your honeyed lips were dripping
The vintage wine of years
Today your memories gripping
(I can fathom your fears)

The dark erased each line
Of age—You were so tender
A while you were just mine
How could I not surrender?

There's little similarity
Between us this I know
Although I saw with clarity
That night amid your glow

I felt not it was wrong
Embracing you—your touch
Left my heart in song
And lifted me so much

I saw you young and fair
Reaching out that night
When you seemed to care
I held you tight

And yes—I'll say I cared
If you cared but slightly
I'll cherish what we shared
And rightly

Katrina Of The Heart

Ah but how her presence was exquisite on the floor!
The dance floor as we moved, moved with us flowing, Ah Katrina
Katrina soft and lovely and a vision on the night
And passing on tommorrow says she'll write me in her flight
How can I tell Katrina I was married though divorced?
She's twenty two I'm twenty three and lived my life much more

Ah Katrina you were yielding and feminine and soft
And made me feel so masculine you flowed with me like wine
You talked and flowed right through my mind, we danced we danced, we danced
I stood so tall; you said I did, and too I was entranced
How can I know my feelings, now, tonight, how can I know?
My mind and soul are reeling and my psyche is aglow

Katrina, I was married though our minds became apart
But justified, oh is it, that I feel this thing inside?
Confused I am because I loved her deeply, yes oh yes
But never did she flow with me like you, I dare confess
And you have never married or had children, dearest lord
The guilt I feel; the stream, I am suggesting that you ford

Ah Katrina, Oh Katrina; was she fated but for me?
Or can she find another who might love her tenderly?
Katrina, oh Katrina, can I start out fresh and new?
Would it be right for all concerned were I to fall for you?
Katrina, Ah Katrina, should you love someone like me?
Katrina, dear Katrina, could you love me—tenderly?

Darling — Our C.

Darling, when we went together
'Neath the sun or filthy weather
You were so God awful pert
I was so—in love it hurt
Never did I touch the ground
With my footsteps always bound
For a creature quiet and shy
When I saw you time did fly
Love, you had such thrilling poise
Like a queen who gently toys
With a man infatuated
Gaining her he gets elated
That is what you did for me
Never was my heart so free
All the night I thought of you
Losing so much sleep it's true
Dreaming of your tender kiss
Scared our love might go amiss
I would drink myself goodnight
With your wine that held me tight
Scheming of the coming day
Hoping you would come my way
Yet my darling, I confess
Still I need your tenderness
And my heart won't be subdued
Though long since I said I do
Always I will need your glow
Darling, yes, I love you so

From Then To Now

Sometimes it is sad to think
I've gone from boyhood in a blink.
Remembrance of the myrtle and the fawn
And wide-eyed innocence are gone.
The world then seemed so compact,
It's boundaries in my mind exact.
The neighbourhood was all I knew,
But, it, the world, and people grew.
So, now my mind's a muddled range
Of deep conceptions marked by change.
And where I'm going mystifies,
Though I see from different eyes.
Loved ones oft have passed away;
Skies once blue seem stagnant gray.
Now I wish I could have grasped
And kept some things so long elapsed
Loved ones left on darkened wings,
Unremittent fateful things.
Aye, I'll know them never more
Though they fill my bosom's core.
Yet, in love, the seasons turned,
From the past my heart's discerned.
And a love life of my own
Tells me, in my love, I've grown.
May I never grow so old
That my heart will not unfold.
I'll not dwell on lonely things.
I will see what loving brings.

First Love

A times comes in a young man's life
When living seems a lesser strife
And virulent vistas in his heart
Are wiled away they soon depart
To leave a gapping hole that's wide
So songbirds singing float inside
And flitter away at his heart strings
Till his heart wings and his heart sings
Where joyful jonquils sprout within
Amid a heart that courses gin
And each and every julep sigh
Gushes as she passes by
Out and over his heart's rim
Intoxicating him

Ballad of Julia

Presently lovingly I reflect
As often on long weary days
Of a time in my youth I recollect
Was a sugar sweet, nectarine Phase

And Julia, a song
Had come like a song sung sweet
And her fondness for me wasn't wrong
She made better the summer heat

She had experience I
Had not had at all, I was callow
But must have seemed nice in her eyes
Julia wasn't shallow

Being a youth and but just thirteen
I rambled in innocence, then
Wet behind the ears and green
But this Julia came and when
She smiled I thought her a queen

Though somehow I sensed a sadness
So far far inside a tear
When imminent turned to gladness
When I was near

I'd told her I thought she was pretty
And the nicest girl I had ever known
But then she talked on of the city
She was from with a wavering tone

She liked me I sensed but she held back
Much of her feelings seemed masked
Somehow I felt I hadn't the knack
To query at all yet I asked

Julia, sometimes, you seem hurt
Why do you seem so quiet?
Inexperience made me overt
Julia still was silent

Like a person of wisdom much more than me
She looked on me with those sad eyes
We walked on to school so silently
I tried to conceal my sighs

I wish to God, somehow, I could have saw
In her eyes the courage she had
Though laden with sorrow she set her jaw
In the presence of this lad

This girl who was deeply troubled within
Who'd born a child out of wedlock
Taken advantage of left in sin
She was, in my presence, a rock

But I had not the insight at all
To offer my faith and a shoulder
To lessen that girl from the pall
Of a grim life all about her

And sadly endearingly I recall
Of the goodness I saw in her
Julia you were twelve feet tall
(As I remember)

www.ingramcontent.com/pod-product-compliance
Ingram Content Group UK Ltd.
Pitfield, Milton Keynes, MK11 3LW, UK
UKHW041431210726
13854UKWH00010B/1851

9 781463 445386